OPAL

OPAL

The Journal of an
Understanding
Heart

OPAL WHITELEY
Adapted by Jane Boulton

Tioga Publishing Company
Palo Alto, California

Opal's Diary was first published in 1920 by the
Atlantic Monthly Press.
This adaptation was first published in 1976 by
Macmillan Publishing Company, Inc.
Published by Tioga Publishing Company, Palo Alto, California.
Copyright © 1984 by Jane Boulton
Cover Design by Andrea Hendrick

Library of Congress Cataloging in Publication Data
Boulton, Jane.
        Opal, the journal of an understanding heart.
        Adaptation of: The Story of Opal/Opal Whiteley.
        Includes index.
1. Whiteley, Opal Stanley, in fiction, drama, poetry, etc.
2. Oregon—Social life and customs—Poetry.
3. Nature—Poetry. I. Whiteley, Opal Stanley.
Story of Opal. II. Title.
PR9199.3.B6206   1984   811'.54   84-2418
ISBN 0-935382-52-6

First Printing 1984
Printed in the United States of America

Distributed by Tioga Publishing Company
Box 50490
Palo Alto, California 94303

        5   6   7   8   9   10

INTRODUCTION

JANE BOULTON

May 1975

This is the unusual diary of a most unusual child who was born just before 1900. Her precocity was to set her apart all her life long and the vividness of her inner life was to bring her both acclaim and misunderstanding.

Before she was five she lost her parents and was given to the wife of an Oregon lumberman. Opal Whiteley—that was the name they gave her—lived in nineteen lumber camps before she was twelve. At that time a foster sister in a childish temper unearthed the diary from its hiding place and tore it into myriad fragments. Opal stored the pitiful scraps in a secret box.

Desperately poor at the age of twenty, Opal brought a nature book she had written to the editor of the Atlantic Monthly Press, Ellery Sedgwick, in hopes of selling it. A fairyland of beasts and blossoms, butterflies and birds, it was quaintly embellished with colored pictures pasted in by hand.

There was little about the book to tempt a business-man, but the girl herself—"something very young and eager and fluttering, like a bird in a thicket"—had a special appeal. After hearing bits of her life story, intrigued by her occasional French words, Sedgwick was moved to ask if she had ever kept a diary. With that Opal burst into tears.

Then, painfully, over nine months, she pieced together the pages written when she was five and six years old. They were published as *The Story of Opal* by Atlantic Monthly Press in 1920.

In this version scenes have been rearranged and characters introduced differently. Except for a few words that are charmingly misspelled, most of the spelling has been corrected. Since the lines seemed like poetry, that is the form I gave them. But the words are Opal's.

OPAL

I

$\mathcal{M}_y$ mother and father are gone.
The man did say they went to heaven
and do live with God,
but it is lonesome without them.

The mama where I live says I am a new sance.
I think it is something grownups
don't like to have around.
She sends me out to bring wood in.
Some days there is cream
to be shaked into butter.
Some days I sweep the floor.
The mama has likes to have
her house nice and clean.

Under the steps lives a toad.
I call him Virgil.

He and I—we are friends.
Under the house live some mice.
They have such beautiful eyes.
I give them bread to eat.

Today the folks are gone away
from the house we do live in.
They are gone a little way away
to the ranch house where
the grandpa does live.
I sit on our steps and print.

I like this house we do live in
being at the edge of the near woods.
So many little people live in the woods.
I do have conversations with them.
I found the near woods first day
I did go explores.

All the way from the other logging camp
in the beautiful mountains
we came in a wagon.
Two horses were in front of us.
They walked in front of us all the way.

When first we were come
we did live with some people in the
ranch house that wasn't builded yet.
After that we lived in a tent,
and often when it did rain

many raindrops came right through the tent.
They did fall in patters on the stove,
and on the floor and on the table.
Too, they did make the quilts
on the bed some damp—
but that didn't matter much
because they soon got dried
hanging around the stove.

From the tent we were come
to this lumber shanty.
It has got a divide in it.
One room we do have sleeps in.
In the other room
we do have breakfast and supper.

Back of the house are some nice woodrats.
The most lovely of them all
is Thomas Chatterton Jupiter Zeus.
He has been waiting in my sunbonnet
long waits while I make prints.
He wants to go explores.
The dog, Brave Horatius, has longings in his eyes.
He wants to go.
In the pig pen I hear Peter Paul Rubens squealing.
We will all go explores.

*O*ne way the road does go
to the house of the girl who has no seeing.

When it gets to her house
it does make a bend
and it does go its way to the blue hills.
I tell her about the trees talking.
I tell her cloud ships are sailing
over the hills in a hurry.

*O*ne way the road does go
to the house of Sadie McKibben.
It doesn't stop when it gets to her house,
but mostly I do.
The freckles on her wrinkled face
are like the Milky Way.
She is awful old—going on forty.
There are cookies in her cookie jar.

Her house is close to the mill by the far woods.
That mill makes a lot of noise.
It can do two things at once.
It makes the noises
and it does saw logs into boards.

Between the brooks are ranch houses.
I have not knowing of the people
that do dwell in them.
But I do know some of their cows
and horses and pigs.
They are friendly folk.

Sometimes I read the books
that Angel Mother and Angel Father did write in.
They tell me about all the great men.
Now I know what to name my favorite mouse.
He is Felix Mendelssohn.

Today was taking-egg day.
One day a week the mama does send me
to take eggs to all the folks hereabouts.
As quick as she did set out the lard pail
with a dozen eggs in it,
I put on my sunbonnet.
It is blue and has a ruffle on it.

Sometimes I wear it on my head,
but most times it hangs back over my shoulders.
Often I carry it over my arm with things in it—
earthworms for baby birds,
bandages for the folks that get hurt,
and mentholatum.
And my friends ride in it.
Sometimes it's a mouse

and sometimes it's a beetle.
Very often it is toads and caterpillars—
only they don't ride
in the sunbonnet at the same time
because I have learned that toads
like caterpillars for breakfast.
A sunbonnet is a very useful thing.

Before I took up the bucket,
I did look long looks at those eggs.
They were so plump and so white.
I think being a hen
must be a very interesting life.
How thrilling it must be to cackle
after one lays an egg.
And it must be a big amount of satisfaction
to have a large number of children
hatch out and follow one about.

When the mama saw me looking looks,
she gave me a shoulder shake
and told me to get a hurry on
and take those eggs to Mrs. Limberger.
Mrs. Limberger is the quite plump wife
of that quite big man
that does live in a quite big house
that is nice,
but not as nice as his lane.

New folks live by the mill.
Dear Love, her young husband does call her.

They are so happy.
But they have been married seven whole months
and haven't got a baby yet.
I pray prayers for Angels
to bring them one real soon.

When I told her, she smiled glad smiles
and kissed me.
Then I did have joy feels all over
and Felix Mendelssohn poked his nose
out of my sleeve.
She gave him a little pat
and I new Dear Love was my friend.

*T*oday was a warm hot day.
It was warm in the morning and hot at noon.
I carried water to the hired men
in the field with a jug.
I got the water out of the pump.
The men were glad.

While I was taking water,
my crow, Lars Porsena, who is very black,
took the thimble from the mama's sewing basket.
She didn't have it.
And she couldn't find it.

She sent me to watch for it everywhere.
I know how Lars Porsena
has a fondness for collecting things

of bright colors—like unto my
fondness for collecting rocks—
so I ran to his hiding place
in the old oak tree.
There I found the mama's thimble.

I got a spanking with a hazel switch
that grows by our back steps.
She said it was as though I'd taken it
because he was my property.
Inside me I couldn't help feeling
she ought to give me thanks
for finding the thimble.

When I feel sad inside
I talk things over with my tree.
I call him Michael Raphael.
It is a long jump from the barn roof into his arms.
I might get my leg or my neck broken
and I'd have to keep still a long time.
So I always say a little prayer
and do jump in a careful way.
It is such a comfort to
nestle up to Michael Raphael.
He is a grand tree.
He has an understanding soul.

After I talked to him and listened to his voice,
I slipped down out of his arms,
but I slid off the wrong limb

and landed in the pig pen
on top of Aphrodite, the mother pig.
She gave a peculiar grunt.

I felt I ought to make it up to her
by taking her for a walk.
I got a piece of clothesline rope.
While I was making a halter for Aphrodite
I took my Sunday-best hair ribbon—
the blue one Uncle Henry gave me—
and put the bow just over her ears.
That gave her a proper look.
When the mama saw us go walking by
she took the bow off the pig.
She put the bow in the trunk.
Me she put under the bed.

By and by—some long time it was—
she took me from under the bed
and did give me a spanking.
She did not have time
to give me a spanking when she
put me under the bed.
After she did it, she sent me
to the ranch house to get milk for the baby.
I walked slow through the oak grove
looking for caterpillars.
I found nine.

When I came to the ranch house
a black cat was sitting on the doorstep.

I have not friendly feelings for that cat.
Day before yesterday I saw him
kill the mother hummingbird.
He knocked her with his paw into the nasturtiums.
I didn't even speak to him.

Just as I was going to knock
on the door for milk,
I heard a voice on the front porch.
I hurried around.
There was Sadie McKibben
with a basket on her arm.
She beamed a smile at me.

Her hands are all brown and cracked
like dried up mud puddles,
but she has an understanding soul.
She has bandages ready
when some of my pets get hurt.

Sadie McKibben walked beside me
when I took the milk home.
When we came near, she took from her basket
wrapping papers and gave them to me to print upon.
Then she kissed me goodbye—
two on the cheeks and one on the nose.

*T*he colic had the baby today
and there was no Castoria for the pains.

There was none because yesterday Pearl*
and I climbed on a chair
and then upon the dresser
and drank up the new bottle of Castoria.
It gave us queer feels.
Pearl lay down on the bed.
I did rub her head.
But she said it wasn't her head—
it was her back that hurt.
Then she said it was her leg that ached.
The mama came in the house then.
She did take Pearl in a quick way
to the grandma at the ranch house.

It was a good time for me
to go away exploring,
but I didn't feel like going.
I just sat on the doorstep.
I did sit there and hold my chin in my hand.
I did have no longings to print.
I only did have longings
not to have those queer feels.

Brave Horatius, my dog, came walking by.
He did make a stop at the doorstep.
He wagged his tail.
That meant he wanted to go
on an exploration trip.

*a foster sister

Lars Porsena flew down from the oak tree.
He did perch on the back of Brave Horatius.
He gave two caws.
That means he wanted to go on an exploration trip.

Felix Mendelssohn crawled into my lap.
I gave him pats.
He cuddled his nose under my curls.
Brave Horatius did wait waits,
but still those queer feels wouldn't go away.
Pretty soon I got awful sick.

*S*ometimes I share my bread and jam
with yellow jackets.
They have a home on a bush
distant from the garden twenty trees and one.
Today I climbed the fence close to their home
with a piece and a half of bread and jam.
The half piece for them
and the piece for myself.
They all wanted to be served at once.

I broke it all into little pieces
and they had a royal feast there on the fence.
Yellow jackets are such interesting fairies
being the world's first paper-makers.

*T*he mama was cutting out biscuits
with the baking powder can.

She put the pan of biscuits
on the wood box back of the stove.
She put a most clean towel over them.
Then she went to gather in the clothes.
I cut little biscuits from the big biscuits.
The mama found me.
She put the thimble back in the drawer.
She put me under the bed.
Here under the bed I now print.

*T*oday near eventime I did lead
the girl who has no seeing
a little way away into the forest
where it was darkness and shadows were.
I led her toward a shadow
that was coming our way.
It did touch her cheeks
with its velvety fingers.
And now she too
does have likings for shadows.
And her fear that was is gone.

After that we turned about to the way
that does lead out of the forest.
And so we went and I did lead her home.
We did hurry because it was most time
for her folks to be there.
Often she does say I mustn't be thereabout
when her folks are thereabout.
I don't be.

$\mathcal{A}$ cornfield is a very nice place.
Some days we children make hair
for our clothespin dolls
from the silken tassels of the corn.
Tonight I walked zigzag across the field
to look for things.
I met two of my mouse friends.
I gave them nibbles of food from my pocket.

Then I saw a man and a woman
coming across the field.
The man was carrying a baby.
I came up to them.
It was Larry and Jean and their baby.
They let me pat the baby's hand
and smooth back its hair.

I do love babies.
When I grow up I want twins
and eight more children.
I want to write outdoor books
for children everywhere.

I remember the first time I saw Larry and Jean
and the bit of poetry he said to her.
They were standing by an old stump
in the lane where the leaves whispered.
Jean was crying.
He patted her on the shoulder.

He said:
"There, little girl, don't cry.
I'll come back and marry you by and by."
And he did.

And the angels looking down from heaven
saw their happiness
and brought them a baby real soon—
when they had been married most five months,
which is very nice
for a baby is such a comfort.

When I went by the barn
I saw a graceful bat
come near unto the barn door.
This is a wonderful world to live in.

In the morning of today
part way to school I met a glad surprise.
There was my dear pig waiting for me.
I gave him three joy pats on the nose

and did call him by name ten times.
I was so glad to see Peter Paul Rubens.

The first time I saw him
was the twenty-ninth of June.
He was little then—a very plump pig—
and wanted to go everywhere I did go.
One day he hurt his nose
and did give such an odd pain squeal
I run a quick run to him.
After that he comes to the kitchen door
and gives the same red ribbon squeal.
He knows that will bring me at once.

This morning when I did start on to school
he gave the same squeal
and came a-following after.
When he was caught up with me he gave a grunt.
A lump came up in my throat.
I couldn't tell him to go back to the pig pen.
So we went along to school together.

School was already took up.
I went in first.
The new teacher told me I was tardy again.
She did look out the door.
There was Peter Paul Rubens.
She did ask me where that pig came from.
I started to tell her all about him
from the very first day.
She did look long looks at me.

She did look those long looks for a long time.
I made pleats in my apron with my fingers.
I made nine on one side
and three on the other side.
When I was through counting the pleats
I did ask her what she was
looking long looks at me for.
She said, "I'm screw tin eyesing you."
I never did hear that word before.
It does have an interesting sound.
I think I will have uses for it.

Then the teacher went back to her desk.
She did call the sixth grade physiology class.
I sat in my seat.
Peter Paul Rubens waited waits at the steps.

It wasn't long until he walked right in.
He did make such a sweet picture
as he did stand in the doorway
looking looks about.
The grunts he gave were such nice ones.
He stood there saying:
"I have come to your school.
What class are you going to put me in?"
They were the same words
I did say on my first day at school.

The children all turned in their seats.
I'm sure they were glad he was in school—
and him talking there in that dear way.

I guess our teacher doesn't have
understanding of pig talk.
She came at him in a hurry with a stick.
When I made interferes
she did send us both home in a quick way.
On the way we dug up many little plants
to plant in my cathedral.
And we had prayers
and came home.

When the cornflowers grow in the fields
I do pick them up,
and make a chain of flowers
for Shakespeare's neck.
Then I do talk to him
about the one he was named for.
He is such a beautiful grey horse
and his ways are ways of gentleness.
Too, he does have likings
like the likings I have
for the blue hills beyond the fields.

Today I did meet Sadie McKibben.
It was nice to see her freckles
and the smiles in her eyes.
She did have me shut my eyes
and she did lay a new blue ribbon in my hand.
It is for Aphrodite, the mother pig.

Now she will have a ribbon all her own
when we go walking down the lane
and to services in my cathedral.
I had hurry feels to go to the pig pen.
I think Sadie McKibben saw the hurrys in my eyes.
She did kiss me goodbye—
one quick kiss.

Then I run quick to show Aphrodite.
I gave her little pats on the nose
and long rubs on the ears.
I did hold it close to her eyes
so she could have seeing of its
beautiful blues like the blues of the sky.
She did grunt thank grunts.
She wanted to go for a walk and wear it.

I did make invest tag ashuns
where the pig pen had a weak place.
It was not any more.
The chore boy has fixed it tight.
I did feel some sad feels
that I could not take her walking
with her nice new blue ribbon on.

While I did feel the sad feels
I did carry bracken ferns
to make her a nice bed.
It brought her feels of where
we went for walks.

Then I went to get the other folks.
Back with me came the dog, Brave Horatius,
and the crow, Lars Porsena,
and the woodrat, Thomas Chatterton Jupiter Zeus,
and the toad, Virgil,
and the mouse, Felix Mendelssohn.
When we were all come
I did climb right into the pig pen
and did tie on Aphrodite's new ribbon.
I sang a little thank song
and we had prayers
and I gave Aphrodite little scratches
on the back with a stick
like she does like.
That was to make up to her
for not getting a walk.

I thought I would go
to the moss box by the old log
to see if the fairies did find my letter.
I walked along the logs
and I went among the ferns.
I did have feels of their gentle movements.

When I came to the box the letter was gone.
Then I did have joy feels all over.
The color pencils—they were come.
There was a blue one and a green one
and a yellow one.

More there were.
I did look looks at them a long time.
It was so nice, the quick way
the fairies did bring them.

I did make a start to go to the mill.
No one does have knowing
of that box but one.
He is the man that wears grey neckties
and is kind to mice.
Sometimes he makes a special fairy wish with me.
All the way along I did feel glad feels
and I had thinks how happy he would be.
Peter Paul Rubens went with me.
He did give a little grunt.
And Brave Horatius came a-following after.

When we were come near the mill
it was near grey-light-time.
The lumbermen were on their way home.
They did whistle as they did go.
Two went side by side,
and three came after
and one came after all.
It was the man that wears grey neckties
and is kind to mice.

Brave Horatius made a quick run to meet him
and I did follow after.
I did have him guess

what the fairies did bring this time.
He guessed a sugar lump for my horse,
William Shakespeare.
I told him it wasn't a right guess.
He guessed some more
but he couldn't guess right.
So I showed them all to him.
He was so surprised.
And he was so glad about it.
He always is.

11

Today I do sit here at my desk
while the children are out for recess time.
I cannot have goings to talk to the trees.
Teacher says I must stay in the whole time.
After our reading lesson
the teacher did ask questions.
First she asked Jimmy to spell horse
and donkey and engine.
He did.
Then she asked Big Jud some things,
and he got up in a slow way
and said, "I don't know"—
like he most always does—
and he sat down.
Then she asked Lola some things
and Lola did tell her all in one breath.

And teacher marked her a good mark in the book
and she gave Lola a smile.
And Lola gave her nice red hair a smooth back
and smiled a smile back at the teacher.

Then the teacher did call my name.
I stood up real quick.
I did have thinks it would be nice
to get a smile from her like Lola got.
The teacher did ask me eight things at once.
"What is a baby pig, a baby deer, a baby horse."
And I did say in a quick way,
"A pig is a cochon.
A deer is a daine.
A horse is a poulain."
Teacher did shake her head and say,
"It is not."
And I did say, "It is."

When I was all through she did say,
"You have them all wrong.
They are not what you said."
And when she said that I did just say,
"They are—they are—they are."

Teacher did say, "Opal, for that
you are going to stay in at recess
today and tomorrow and the next day.
You will be an egg sam pull
for all the other children in our school."

They are out at play.
It is a most long recess.
But I know a pig is a cochon.
A mouse is a mulot.
A duck is a canard.
Angel Father always did call them so.
He knows.
But no one hereabouts does call things
by the names that Angel Father did.
I do have lonesome feels.

Outside the window I have hearings
of the talk of girls.
They talk of what they want.
Martha wants a bow.
I don't have seeings why she wants another one.
Both her braids were tied back
this morning with a new bow
the color of the blossoms of camarine.

Lola wants a white silk dress
with a little ruffle around the neck
and one around the sleeves.
She says she will be a great lady then.
And she says all the children will gather around
her and sing when she has her white dress on.
And while they sing
she will stretch out her arms
and bestow her blessing on all the people
like the deacon does
in the church at the mill town.

On my way coming home from school
I did see four grey squirrels and two chipmunks.
By the side of the river goes the railroad track.
It has a squeaky voice,
but it does have shining rails
that do stretch away and away
like a silver ribbon
that came from the moon in the night.

I go a-walking on these rails.
I get off when I do hear
the approaches of the dinky engine.
On every day excepting Sunday
comes and goes the logging train.
It goes to the camps
and it does bring back cars of logs
and cars of lumber to take to the mill town.

Today I saw a tramper coming on the tracks.
This tramper—he did have a big roll on his back—
and he walked steps on the ties
in a slow tired way.
When I was come more near
I did have thinks he might have hungry feels.
Most trampers do.

I took the lid off my lunch pail.
There was just a half piece
of bread and butter left.
I was saving that to make divides

between Peter Paul Rubens and Aphrodite
and Felix Mendelssohn.
I looked at the tramper.
Then I did have little feels
of the big hungry feels
he might be having.
I ran a quick run to catch up with him.
He was glad for it.
He ate it in two bites.

Today the grandpa dug potatoes in the field.
I followed along after.
I picked them up and piled them in piles.
Some of them were very plump.
And all the time I was picking up potatoes
I did have conversations with them.
To some potatoes I did tell about
my hospital in the near woods
and all the little folk in it
and how much prayers and songs
and mentholatum helps them to have well feels.

To other potatoes I did talk about my friends—
how the crow, Lars Porsena,
does have a fondness for collecting things,
how Aphrodite, the mother pig, has a fondness
for chocolate creams,
how my dear pig, Peter Paul Rubens, wears a
little bell coming to my cathedral service.

Potatoes are very interesting folks.
I think they must see a lot
of what is going on in the earth.
They have so many eyes.
Too, I did have thinks
of all their growing days
there in the ground,
and all the things they did hear.

And after, I did count the eyes
that every potato did have,
and their numbers were in blessings.

I have thinks these potatoes growing here
did have knowings of star songs.
I have kept watch in the field at night
and I have seen the stars
look kindness down upon them.
And I have walked between the rows of potatoes
and I have watched
the star gleams on their leaves.

*T*he mama sent me to Elsie's to get
the tidy she was crocheting
that she did forget and leave there.
When I came to her house,
Elsie was trotting on her knee
that dear baby boy the angels brought her.
She was singing:

> *"Gallop-a-trot*
> *Gallop-a-trot*
> *This is the way the gentlemen ride.*
> *Gallop-a-trot."*

She tossed her head as she did sing,
and the joy light danced in her eyes.
Elsie has not been married long.
She has only one baby.
She has much liking for it.
Elsie is a very young girl—
a very young girl to be married,
the mama says.

I have thinks it must be wonderful
happiness to be married.
I have seen the same joy-light in the eyes
of her tall young husband.
It is there much when he is come home
at eventide from work in the woods.
Then she does have many kind words
and kisses for him.

He has adoors for her,
and too he has a pumpadoor that he
smooths back with vaseline.

While I was coming home I saw a grey board.
I did turn it over.
Under the board were five silk bags.
They were white
and they did feel lumps.
I know baby spiders will come out of them
when spring days come
because last year I found bags like these
and this year in the spring
baby spiders walked out.
They were very fidgety youngsters.

I heard the mama calling.
I put the board back the way it was.
She did send me in a hurry to the woodshed.
She wanted two loads of wood.
The first load I brought in a hurry.
The second load I brought not so.
I did pick up all the sticks my arms could hold.

I looked long looks at them.
I did have thinks about the tree
they all were before they got chopped up.
I did wonder how I would feel
if I was a very little piece of wood
that got chopped out of a very big tree.

I did think that it would have hurt my feelings.
I felt the feelings of the wood.
They did have a very sad feel.

Then the mama did come up
behind me with a switch.
She said while she did switch,
"Stop your meditations."
And while she did switch, I did drop the wood.
Then I did pick them up with care
and put them in the woodbox back of the stove.
All the time I was humming a little song.
It was a goodbye song to the sticks.

When the churning was done
and the butter was come,
the mama did lift all the little lumps
of butter out of the churn.
Then she did pat them together in a big lump,
and this she put away in the butter box
in the woodshed.
When she went to lay herself down to rest
on the bed she did call me to rub her head.
I like to rub the mama's head,
for it does help the worry lines to go away.
Often I rub her head,
and I do think it is very nice to help
people have what they do have longings for.

At night the wind goes walking in the field
talking to the earth voices there.
I did follow her down potato rows.
And her goings made ripples on my nightgown.
The lovely woodrat, Thomas Chatterton Jupiter Zeus,
did cuddle more closely in my arms.
And Brave Horatius followed after.

While I was listening to the voices of the night,
Brave Horatius did catch the corner
of my nightgown in his mouth
and did pull in a most hard way
to go back to the house we live in.
He barks when he thinks it is going-home-time.
I listen.
Sometimes I go back and he goes with me.
Sometimes I go on and he goes with me.
He knows most all the poetry
I have told to the potatoes at night.

Then I did think as how the next day would be
the borning day of Louis Philippe, roi de France.
First I did sing:
"Sanctus, sanctus, sanctus, Dominus Deus."
Then I did sing three times over:
"Gloria Patri, et Filio, et Spiritu Sancto.
Hosanna in excelsis."

All the potatoes were in rows.
One row was forty-four and one was sixty.

A choir with a goodly number of folks in it—
all potato folks wearing brown robes.
Then I did sing one "Ave Maria."

Today I did make a choir robe for Alfred Tennyson.
In my book eighty-three were his years.
Brave Horatius did have seeing
as how I was bringing potatoes to the choir.
And so he did bring some—
one at a time in his mouth.
He is a most helpful dog.

I was just going to sing
"Deo Gratias, Hosanna in excelsis"
when Brave Horatius barked three times.
The chore boy did have steps behind me.
He gave me three shoulder shakes.
He did tell me to get a hurry on me,
and get those potatoes picked up.
I so did in quick time.
Brave Horatius did follow after.
He gave helps.
He did lay the potatoes in the piles.

When near-grey-light-time was come,
the chore boy went from the field.
When most-dark-time was come,
Brave Horatius and I so went.

I did have thinks about
Thomas Chatterton Jupiter Zeus—
about his nose, its feels.
Some way he got his nose too near
that trap they set for rats in the barn.
So now he is in my hospital
and his nose is getting well.

For breakfast he has some of my oatmeal.
For dinner he has some of my dinner.
For supper I carry to him corn in a jar lid.
Sadie McKibben gives me enough
mentholatum to put on his nose
seven times a day.
Today when I took him in my arms
he did cuddle up.
It means he is growing better.

Too, he gave his cheese squeak.
That made me have lonesome feels.

The mama did say, "Don't you dare
carry any more cheese out to that rat."
And so I do not carry any out.
But when the mama is gone
I carry Thomas Chatterton Jupiter Zeus
into the kitchen and cut a piece for him.

Today the mama is at home
so there is no cheese for my lovely woodrat.
I did go to Sadie McKibben's
so she might have knowings of the nose improvement
of Thomas Chatterton Jupiter Zeus.
When I came near to him
he did squeak more of his cheese squeaks.
It was most hard—having hearing
of him and not having cheese for him.
I could hardly keep from crying.
He is a most lovely woodrat
and all his ways are ways of gentleness.
He is just like the mama's baby—
when he squeaks he does have expects
to get what he squeaks for.

When I was talking to Sadie McKibben
he began again and went on
and did continue so.
I did cuddle him up more close in my arms.
I just couldn't keep from crying.
His cheese longings are like my longings
for Angel Mother and Angel Father.

Sadie McKibben did wipe her hands on her apron.
She did have askings what was the matter.
"Oh, Sadie McKibben, it's his cheese squeak."
And she said not a word
but she did go in a quick way to her kitchen.

Now he has enough cheese for
two breakfasts and four dinners.
Then she did smooth back my curls
and did give me three kisses—
one on each cheek and one on the nose.
She smiled her smile upon us
and we were most happy
and we did go from her house to the cathedral.
There I did have a thank service
for the goodness of God
and the goodness of Sadie McKibben
and the lovely piece of cheese
that did bring peace
to the dear Thomas Chatterton Jupiter Zeus.

I did have remembers as how the mama
did say at morning-time
there was much work to be done before even-time.
I made a start at the works.
I did feed the chickens
and there was much wood to bring in
and baby clothes to wash
and ashes to empty from the stove.

These four things I did.
The mama and Pearl
and the baby went to the house of Elsie.

I looked looks about to see what other
works did have needs to be done.
I had remembers that when the papa
went away to work this morning
he said he did not have time to cut the ham.
If he is too busy in the morning
to get a thing done
it mostly don't get done
when he comes home from work at night
because he has so tired feels.

I had thinks I better help with the ham.
I went out to the woodshed.
I piled the wood high enough
so I could stand on tiptoes
and reach the flour sack the ham was tied in.
I pulled and pulled,
but it wouldn't come down.
I didn't have knows what I was going to do.
Pretty soon, by having concentration of my thinks,
I thought of a way.
I got the scissors
and cut the bottom out of the sack.
That ham came down right quick.
It landed on the woodpile.

I dragged it up on the chopping block.
Then I got the butcher knife
from its place in the kitchen drawer.
I went to work.
That knife didn't make moves
like the moves in the hands of the papa.

I made begins.
Then I made a stop to rest.
Then I made the knife go some more.
I made another stop to rest.
Pretty soon a slice of ham
landed on the woodpile.
I held it up to take a look.
I did feel such proud feels.
I had cut it in such a nice way.
It had frills around
and holes in between
just like Elsie's crochet doily.
After I did hang that slice of ham
on a nail by the door,
I did cut another slice
when I did hear a heavy step.

There was a tramper by the woodshed door.
He had not gentle looks
like some trampers have.
His beard did grow in the hobo way,
and he had no neatness.
He stood there looking at that ham,
and he did walk right into the woodshed.

He had asking if the mama was at home.
"No, she is not. She is at the house of Elsie."
Then he says, "I guess I'll take this
ham along with me."

I almost lost my breathing.
I did remember all the days
the papa has plans for ham
at breakfast and dinner and supper.
So I just sat on the ham and spread
my blue calico apron out over it.
And while I sat I did pray
to God to keep it safe
for breakfasts and dinners and suppers
of the papa and the mama.

The tramper looked queer looks at me.
He came a little more near.
I did pray on.
And God in his goodness
sent answers to my prayer in a quick way.
Brave Horatius came from somewhere.
He made a stop at the door.
He looked a look in.
He gave a growl.
Then he went at that tramper.
He did grab him by his ragged pants.
The tramper gave a squeal of pain
and shook his leg.
Then he did go in a hurry away.
Brave Horatius followed after.

Now I have thinks about trampers.
How they do differ.
A week ago one did come to the door.
He gave a gentle rap.
He had a clean sad face
and a kind look in his eyes.
The man said he was on his way
to the camp to get work.
The roll on his back was heavy.
I straightway did go
and get my bowl of bread and milk
and gave it to him.
He ate it in a hungry way
like Brave Horatius when we are back
from a long explore trip.
Then, when the man did eat all the bread and milk,
he did split some wood in the woodshed
and pile it up in a nice way.

When he did go he said,
"The Lord's blessing be with you, child."
I said, "It is."
And I did tell him
"We have a cathedral in the woods.
At eventime when we have prayers
we will pray that you get work at the camp."

And at eventime we did.
And Peter Paul Rubens
did grunt Amen in between times.

Now every day we do pray
for the man that was hungry
and had a kind look in his eyes.

*T*oday again the mama did go to the house of Elsie.
Before she did go she told me
the do's to do while she was gone:
to keep the fire going
and to tend the baby,
to fix its bottle
and to mind it all the time.
Then she shut the door and locked it
and went on her way.
I did watch her out the window.
Then I did put some more wood on the fire.

There are no rows and rows and rows
of books in this house
like Angel Mother and Angel Father had.
There is only three books here.
One is a cook book
and one is a doctor book
and one is a almanac.
They are all on top of the cupboard
most against the top of the house.

The alarm clock does set on the shelf.
At night-time it sets on a chair
by the bed the mama and papa sleep in.

It is so the papa will be made awake
early in the morning.

I did look out the front window.
There are calf tracks by our front door.
Elizabeth Barrett Browning waited yesterday
while I did get her sugar lumps.
I think she will grow up to be a lovely cow.
Her mooings now are very musical
and there is poetry in her tracks.
She does make such dainty ones.
When they dry up I dig them up and save them.
I take them out of the drawer
and look at them
and think:
"this way passed Elizabeth Barrett Browning."

After, I did look looks out the back window.
William Shakespeare and the others
were pulling logs.
Rob Ryder was trying to make them go more fast.
Horses have to pull so hard
when they pull logs in.
Sometimes they have tired looks,
and when they come in from work
I go to the barn.
I rub their heads
to make the tireds go away.

While I did watch the horse
the baby had wakeups.

I went to sing her to sleep.
Raindrops were beginning
to come down from the sky.
Their coming was in a gentle way.
I had longings to be out with them.
I so do like to feel raindrops
patter on my head
and I like to run runs
and hold out my hands to meet them.
When I grow up I am going to write
a book about a raindrop's journey.

Now I sit here and I print.
The baby sleeps on.
The wind comes creeping in under the door.
It calls, "Come, come petite Françoise, come."
It calls me to go exploring.
I listen—but I cannot go.

$\mathcal{N}ow$ are come the days of leaves.
They talk with the wind.
I hear them tell of their borning days.
They whisper of the hoods they wear.
Today they talk of the time
before their borning days.
They tell how they were a part of the earth
and the air before their tree-borning days.
In grey days of winter
they go back to earth again.
But they do not die.

I saw a silken cradle in a hazel branch.
It was cream with a hazel leaf
halfway around it.
I put it to my ear and I did listen.
It had a little voice.
It was not a tone voice.
It was a heart voice.
While I did listen, I did feel its feels.
It has lovely ones.

I did hurry to the house of the girl
who has no seeing
so she might know its feels
and hear its heart voice.
She does so like to feel things.
She has seeing by feels.

One day I told her about trees talking.
Then she did want to know about the voices,
and now I do help her to hear them.
And too I tell her about Comparer
that Angel Father did teach me to play
and I show her the way.

When I came near the barn I thought
of Peter Paul Rubens.
Cathedral service would be good for his soul.
I went inside to get his little bell
and did put it on him.

There was a time when there was no little bell.
That was before one day I did say
to the man that wears grey neckties
and is kind to mice,
"I do have needs of a little bell
for my lovely pig to wear to church."
Now Peter Paul Rubens always knows
he is going to the cathedral
when I put that little bell around his neck.
It does make lovely silver tinkles
as he goes walking down the aisle.

Tonight we did go and with us
Elizabeth Barrett Browning.
I prayed for a long time with prayers
for the goodness of us all.
I forgot all about home.

The mama, she spanked me
and put me under the bed.
And all this nice long time
light is come to here
from the lamp on the kitchen table—
light enough so I can make prints.
I am happy.

At breakfast time I take wheat to the chickens.
I strew it on the ground for them in swings.
When I do swing it a long swing
the wheat goes far.
When I swing it a short swing
it goes only a little ways.
Today I did swing my arm four long swings
and three short swings
and two more long swings.
The chickens were glad to have it so.
They did pick up that wheat in a hurry-way.

I got the lard pail that does
have my lunch in it.
While I was putting on my jacket
the mama did tie a new piece of asfiditee
around my neck to keep me from having disease.
It was a big piece of asfiditee.

It didn't stay a big piece very long.
I divided it with my animal friends.
Now each one of us has a bit of asfiditee

tied around our necks
so we will not catch sickness.
I called Brave Horatius to give him some
but he did not answer and he did not come.

When I got to the school,
teacher was standing there in the door.
She was looking far-off looks
in a way that does lead to the river.
I thought maybe she was having dream-thoughts.
I was just going to walk past her,
when she turned me about.
She felt the outside of my apron pocket,
but I didn't bring my toad to school today.

On the way home I came to the field.
Elizabeth Barrett Browning was at the pasture bars.
There was lonesome feels in her mooings.
I went and put my arm around her neck.
It is such a comfort to have a friend near
when lonesome feels do come.

I have wonders where is Brave Horatius.
He comes not at my calling.
Two days he is now gone.
For him I go on searches.
I go the three roads that go the three ways.
On and on I go.
I call and call.

Into the woods beyond the river I go.
I listen.
The sounds that were in time of summer
are not now.
Brave Horatius is not there.
I go to the house of the girl who has no seeing.
But I have no seeing of my Brave Horatius.

The man that wears grey neckties
and is kind to mice
keeps a watch by the mill,
but these two days he has no seeing
of Brave Horatius.
I have wonders where he can be.
Every time I see the chore boy he does sing,
"There was a little dog and his name was Rover,
and when he died, he died all over,
and—when—he—died—he—died—all—over."
The last part he does wail in a most long way.

I have not listenings to what that boy says.
I go on.
I pray on.
I look and look for Brave Horatius.
I go four straight ways
and come back four different ways.
Lonesome feels are everywhere.

In the morning of today when I was looking
I did meet with the father of Lola,

and I did ask if he had seen my Brave Horatius.
He had no seeing of him, but he did ask me
where I was going on my searches.
I did tell him to the Forest de Montmorency
and to the Orne and Yonne and Rille.
When I did tell him so he did laugh.
Most all the folks do laugh at the names
I do call places hereabout.
They most all do excepting Sadie McKibben.
She smiles and smooths out my curls and says,
"Name 'em what ye are a mind to, dearie."
She promised she will ask everybody
that does go by her house.

All my friends do feel lonesome feels
for Brave Horatius.
Lars Porsena, the crow,
hardly has knowing what to do.
Peter Paul Rubens did have going with me
three times on searches,
but today the pig pen fence was fixed most tight.
I couldn't unfix it with a hammer,
so he couldn't go with me.

I did start on.
He did grunt grunts to go.
I did feel more sad feels.
I do so like to have him go explores with me.
Today I did go on, and did come back
to give him more goodbye pats on the nose.

Four times I did so,
and did tell him when Brave Horatius is found
we will come soon to his pen.

I was not far when the mama
did call me to tend the baby.
When sleeps was upon the baby,
I lay me down to sleep,
for tired feels was upon me.
Now I feel not so.
I have been making prints.
The mama is gone with the baby
to the house of Elsie.
I go now again to seek for my Brave Horatius.

A little way I went. A long way I went.
When I was come part way back again,
I climbed upon the old grey fence made of rails.
I sat there until I saw the shepherd
bringing down the sheep from the blue hills.
When he was come in sight,
I went up to meet him and all the sheeps.
And when I was come near unto them
I did have seeing there by the shepherd's side
my Brave Horatius.
I was full of glad feels.
Brave Horatius showed his glad feels with his tail.
And he did look fond looks
at the flock of sheep.
I so did too.

In the flock was Bede of Jarrow,
and Alfric of Canterbury.
I did give to each and every one
a word of greeting
as I did walk among the flock.
And there were others that
I had not yet given names.
And last of them all—last of all the flock
was Dallan Forgaill.

When we were come a little way
the shepherd did ask me again
what were the names
I did call his sheep,
and I told him all over again.
And he did say them after me.
And he did ask me where I
did have gettings of these names.
And I did tell him from the two books
that Angel Mother and Angel Father
did write in.

We went on.
Pretty soon I did tell him
while he was gone away to the blue hills
I did choose for him another name.
He did have wantings to know
what the other name was.
I did tell him "Aidan of Iona come from Lindisfarne."
He liked it. I told him I did too.
We went on. We did have talks.

When we were come near unto the lane I did say,
"Goodbye, Aidan of Iona come from Lindisfarne.
I am glad you and the flock are come."
He gave my curls a smooth back and he said,
"Goodbye, little one."

Then Brave Horatius and I went in a hurry
to the pig pen to show the friends that he was back.

III

Yesterday the mama let me go off to the woods
all day after my morning's work was done.
Lars Porsena went with me.
Part of the time the crow
perched on my shoulder
and then he would ride on the dog's back.
Felix Mendelssohn rode in my apron pocket.
Elizabeth Barrett Browning followed after.

We had not gone far
when we heard an awful squeal.
I felt cold all over.
Then I did have knowings why the mama
had let me start to the woods
without a scolding.
It was butchering day.
And I ran a quick run
to save my dear Peter Paul Rubens,

but already he was dying—
and he died with his head in my lap.

I sat there feeling dead too
until my knees were all wet with blood
from the throat of dear Peter Paul Rubens.
After I changed my clothes
and put the bloody ones in the rain barrel,
I did go to the woods to look for the soul
of Peter Paul Rubens.
I didn't find it, but I think in spring
I will find it among the flowers.
Today when Brave Horatius and I
went through the woods,
we did feel his presence near.

When I was back from the woods
they made me grind sausage,
and every time I did turn the handle
I could hear that little pain squeal
Peter Paul Rubens always gave
when he did want me
to come where he was at once.

When I woke up this morning
there were pictures on the windowpanes.
By and by the fire in the stove
made the room warm
and the pictures went away.

When I did have my breakfast
the mama did send me
to take eggs to the ranch house.

The outdoors did have coldness.
It made my fingers have queer feels.
And my nose felt like I didn't have any.
Brave Horatius followed after me.
He did put his nose against my hand for a pat.
I gave him two.
One was for him and one
was for Peter Paul Rubens that was.
Every now and then I did stop
to break the ice on the mud puddles.
Today water won't come out of the pump.
The pump handle won't go up and down.
The grandpa said it froze in the night.

I saw the black cat by the barn.
On cold nights I have given that cat
long rubs on its back,
and sparks have come.
I did have thinks about sparky things.
Cats are sparky on cold days.
Rocks are sparky—flint ones—
when you give them a thump.
Stoves are sparky on cold days.
The chore boy says some people are sparky.
He doesn't know what he is talking about.

*T*oday I did teeter the baby on the bed.
I did sing to her:
"Maintenant est hiver,
Le ciel est gris,
Le champ est tranquille,
Les fleurs dorment,
Maintenant est hiver."
[*Winter is here.*
The sky is grey.
The earth is still.
The flowers are sleeping.
Winter is here.]

Then she did kick many kicks in the air.
I did tickle her toes.
She has likes for it.
The baby has likes for many things.
She has likes to sit up on the bed.
And likes to make bubbles with her mouth
and stick her foot in her mouth.
She does like to rattle all the rattles
the grandma and Elsie bring.
This baby likes to be rocked
and when it is awake it wants to be
singed to and carried about.
It has satisfaction looks on its face
for a little time when it gets what it wants.
Soon it does have more wants.

I tied bits of bread
on the branches of the trees.
Too, I tied on popcorn kernels.
They looked like snow-flowers
blooming on the fir trees.
The birds will be glad for them.
I feel the hungry feels the birds are having.
Some have likes for different things.
Little grey one of the black cap
has likes for suet.
Every time I do meet this new old bird
I do say, "I have happy feels
to see you, black cap."

Today there was greyness everywhere—
grey clouds in the sky
and grey shadows above the canyon.
And all the voices were grey.
And Felix Mendelssohn was grey
and down the road I did meet a grey horse—
and his greyness was like the greyness
of William Shakespeare.

Elsie has a brand new baby
and all the things that go with it.
There's a pink fleur on its baby brush
and a pink bow on its quilt.

The angels brought the baby
last night in the night.
I have been to see it a goodly number of times.
Most everything I start to do,
I went aside before I did get through
to take peeps at the darling baby.

The baby is a beautiful baby.
It does have much redness of face
from coming a long way in the cold last night.
Maybe it was the coldness of the night
that did cause the angels to make the mistake.
They stopped at the wrong house.
I'm quite sure this is the very baby
I have been praying for the angels
to bring to Dear Love.

I better tell Elsie as how this baby isn't hers
before she gets too fond of it.
She so likes to cuddle it now.
Both morning and afternoon I did put off
going to tell her about it.
I did wait most until eventime.
Then I couldn't keep still any longer.

Mrs. Limberger that was staying with Elsie
wouldn't let me come in the door
to see the baby again
because she has opinions that nineteen times
is fully enough to be seeing a baby

on the first day of its life on earth.
So I went and got a woodbox off the porch
and I did go around to the bedroom window.

I stood on the woodbox and made tappings
on the windowpane.
Elsie did have hearings.
She did turn her head on the pillow.
She gave nods for me to come in.
I pushed the window a push
enough so I could squeeze in.
Then I sidled over to the bed.

Elsie did look so happy with the baby.
I did swallow a lump in my throat.
She looked kind smiles at me.
I did not like to bring disturbs to her calm.
I just stood there making pleats
in my blue calico apron.
I did have thinks of Dear Love
and the house without a baby
by the mill by the far woods.

Then I felt I couldn't wait any longer.
I just said, "I know you are going
to have a disappoint, Elsie,
but I have got to tell you—
this baby isn't yours.
It's a mistake.
It really belongs to Dear Love

in that most new, most little house
by the mill by the far woods.
It's the one I've been praying
the angels to bring her."

Just when I was all out of breath from telling her,
there did come the heavy step of Mrs. Limberger.
Elsie did say in a gentle way,
"Come to me early in the morning
and we will talk the matter over."
Then I did go out the window.

From there I did go to talk with Michael Raphael.
He does so understand.
All troubles that do trouble me
I do talk over with him.
While I was telling him about the mistake
of the angels, I did hear a little voice.
It was a baby voice.
It did come from the barn.

It wasn't in the haystack.
It seemed to come from way below.
I slid down to the manger
of the gentle Jersey cow.
I thought she was in the pasture,
but there she was in the barn.
And with her was a dear new baby calf.

When I did ask the ranch folks
they did say it was brought

in the night last night.
I have thinks the same angel that did bring
the new baby to the house of Elsie
did bring also in her other arm
that baby calf to the gentle Jersey cow.

Tonight I will pick out a name
from the books Angel Mother
and Angel Father did write in.

*E*arly on the morning of today
I did go to the house of Elsie.
I did rap gentle raps on the door
and the young husband of Elsie
did come to raise the latch.
When the door did come open
I did have seeing that his black pumpadoor
did shine more than most times
and all the vaseline was gone from the jar
that sets on the kitchen shelf.
I did tell him how Elsie did say
for me to come early this morning.
And before he did have time for answers,
Elsie did have hearing in the other room.
She did call me to come in.

In I went.
The baby was beside her.
It was all wrapped in a blanket
so it couldn't have seeings out the window

how the raindrops was coming down so fast.
The young husband of Elsie
did look fond looks at that blanket.
I did begin to have fears
he did have thinks it was his baby.

Elsie did unwrap the blanket from its red face.
Elsie did say, "See its long hair."
And I did have seeing.
It wasn't long though, not more than an inch.
It was most black.
And its eyes—they were dark.
It did have prefers to keep them shut.
Elsie did say,
"Now about what we were talking yesterday:
next time you go to the house of Dear Love
have seeing of the color of her eyes and hair
and also of her husband's.
I hardly think this baby's hair and eyes
are like theirs.
And maybe it is where it does belong."
"I feel sure about that," said her young husband.
But I had not feels so.

*S*ome days there is cream to be shaked into butter.
The mama does have me to make the handle go
up and down a lot of times in the churn.
This makes the butter come.
When there is only a little cream

to be shaked into butter,
then the mama has me to shake it
to and fro in a glass jar.
Sometimes it gets awfully heavy
and my arms do get ache feels up and down.

It was so today.
I gave it many shakes
and I was having hopes it soon would come.

After some long time
when it was most come,
the lid come off and it all shaked out.
The mama did have cross feels.
After I did give the floor washes and mop ups
where the splashes of buttermilk did jump
then the mama put me out the door
and told me to stay out of her way.
I so did.

I straightway did go in a hurry
to the house of Dear Love
by the mill by the far woods.
Many raindrops were coming in a hurry.
When I was come to the house
she was there and he was there.
Her eyes were light blue
and her hair was most cream.
Her husband's eyes were blue
and he has red hair.

I saw.
And I had sad feels.
Dear Love did take me to a chair.
I felt lumps come up in my throat.
She did take off my shoes to dry my feet.

Then she did take me on her lap
and she did ask me what was the matter.
I just did tell her all about it.
How I had been praying for the angels
to bring a baby real soon to them—
and how sad feels I did feel because
they didn't have a baby yet.

Her husband did smile a quiet smile at her
and roses did come on her cheeks.
And I did have thinks
that they did have thinks that the baby
the angels did bring to Elsie
was their baby.

Then I did give them careful explanations
as how I too did have thinks it was their baby
the angels did bring to Elsie,
and as how I did have thinks so yesterday
and last night and right up until now
when I did come and have seeings
of their blue eyes and his red hair.
I did tell them as how this baby
couldn't be theirs because it has

most dark hair and most dark eyes—
like the eyes and the hair of the
husband of Elsie.

Angels do have a goodly amount of wisdom.
They do bring to folks babies
that are like them.
To mother sheeps they do bring lambs.
To mother bats they bring twin bats.
And after I did tell them
it couldn't be their baby,
I did tell them
not to have disappoints too bad
because I am going to pray on—
and maybe she will get a baby next week.

Her young husband did walk over to the window
and look out long looks.
I have thinks he was having wonders
if the quilt they bring with it
will have a blue bow or a pink bow.
I think blue bows will look nicer
with red hair than pink bows.
I have thinks I better put that in my prayers.

By and by, when my feets were dry,
they did put my shoes on and lace them up.
They did want me to stay to dinner,
but I did have feels I must hurry
back to Elsie and tell her

that the baby was hers.
She might be having anxious feels about it.
When I did say goodbye,
they did give me two apples,
one for William Shakespeare
and one for Elizabeth Barrett Browning.

As I did go in hurry steps
to the house of Elsie,
the mama did call me to mind the baby.

I did not have goings to school today
for this is wash day
and the mama did have needs of me at home.
There was baby clothes to wash.
The mama does say that is my work
and I try to do it in the proper way
she does say it ought to be done.
It does take a long time
and all the time it is taking
I do have longings to talk to Elsie
and I do have longings
to go on exploration trips.

I do want to go talk with William Shakespeare
where he is pulling logs in the near woods.
And I do want to talk with the lovely calf,
Elizabeth Barrett Browning,
and I do want to play in the pasture
with Peter Paul Rubens.

When the clothes of the baby were most white,
I did bring them again to the wash bench.
Then there was the chickens to feed
and the stockings were to rub.
Stockings do have needs of many rubs.
That makes them clean.

While I did do the rubs
I did sing little songs to the grasses
that do grow about our door.

Then there was the baby to tend.
I did sing it songs of songs
that Angel Mother did sing to me.
And sleeps came upon the baby.
But she is a baby that does have
wakeups between times.
Today she had a goodly number.

*T*he time came when I could go to Elsie's.
As quick as her young husband did open the door
I did walk right in.
She smiled glad smiles
when I told her it was hers.
It must have been an immense amount of relief—
her not knowing it was really her own baby.

And then I turned around to tell her husband
it was theirs. He just said,
"I knew it was mine."

And he looked fond looks
at the blanket it was wrapped in.
I have feels now it is nice for them to have it.
And it is good they will not have to give it up—
being as it matches them.

Angels do have a goodly amount of wisdom.
This is a wonderful world to live in.

On the way home from school
I did meet with Sadie McKibben
and it was very nice to see her freckles.
She gave me a kiss on my nose
and smoothed back my curls
and shook my hand.
When she so did, Felix Mendelssohn
did poke his nose out the cuff.
He made a quick run up my arm
and settled down on my shoulder.
He is a very quick-running mouse.

She asked if that was all my friends
I did take to school today.

Then I lifted up my apron
and did show her Virgil.
He was riding in a pocket in my underskirt.
Sadie McKibben thought she would
have to be getting me a little basket
to carry them in.

She is going to speak to the man who
wears grey neckties and is kind to mice.
I have thinks to be carried in a warm basket
will please the souls of all the little folk
that do go walking with me.
It will be almost as nice as to ride
in the pockets of the papa's big coat.
I will put pockets in the basket
and divides so there will be little rooms.
I will let them have their turns
riding to school in my basket.

When I did get home Rob Ryder was there.
I haven't been near unto him since
I did bite his hand the other day.
The mama tried to make me say how sorry
I am but I am not a bit sorry—
and I wouldn't say so.
If I got a chance I'd bite him again
for laying that big whip to the back
of William Shakespeare when
he doesn't pull logs fast enough.
To pull those logs he does his very best.

When he was gone away, the mama
did spank me most hard with the hairbrush.
Then she put me out the door.
And I did go and talk with Michael Raphael.

*A*fter I did dishtowel all the dishes
we did use in the breakfast meal,
the mama did send me to get barks
for the warming stove.
While I was getting barks
I did stop to screwtineyes
the plump wiggles that were under all the barks.
They will grow and change into beetles.
I have seen them do so.
I have taken them from the barks
and kept them in the nursery
while they did change.

After barks I did go my way to school.
I made stops where the willows grow.
I love to touch fingers with willows.
Each pussy willow baby
did wear a grey silk tricot.
He did look warm.
I did have talks with them for a time.
I was quite late to school.
Teacher made me to stand in the corner
with my face to the wall.

I looked looks out the window.
I had seeing of little plant folks
just peeping out of the earth
to see what they could see.
I did have thinks it would be nice
to be one of them
and then grow up and have a flower
and bees a-coming and seed-children at fall time.

When teacher did send me to my seat
to get my slate for arithmetic
I did put Virgil in my desk.
There was room enough for a toad
to take nice little hops.

But while I was having recites
he hopped a little hop too far
and he fell out of my desk.
I had quivers and it was hard
to pay attentions to arithmetic.

When our lessons were done
I made a quick go to my seat.
I looked for him.
He was not there.
I looked more looks.

He was rows away where Lola has her sitting.
I had such anxious feels about him.
Lola had seeing.

She made a reach over.
She picked him up in a gentle way.
She put him in her apron pocket.
She asked teacher if she could get a drink
from the wrap room.
She went.
She made a come-back down our row
and she put her hand in my pocket.
She went on to her seat.
Virgil was back again in my apron pocket.
I felt an immense amount
of satisfaction feels.

A man was riding on his horse.
It is so much joy.
I feel the feels the horse does feel
when he puts each foot to the ground.
It would be nice to go a long way on explores.
William Shakespeare was in the lane.
He is a listen horse.
I gave him pats on the nose
and I talked to him about it.
I made a climb on a stump
and did get up
on the back of William Shakespeare.

We went the way of the river.
Long time ago this road
did have a longing to go across the river.

Some wise people did have understandings.
They did build a bridge to go across.
We did watch the water splash itself
against the legs of the bridge.
The bridge did make squeaks
as we went across.

In a big tree was a bunch of mistletoe.
I stood on tiptoe on the back
of William Shakespeare to reach up to it.
I could reach a reach to one limb.
I put my arms around it and had a swing.
But when I was ready
to stand on William Shakespeare again,
he was not there.
He was gone on a little way.
I had wonders what to do.

There was most too many rocks
to drop down on.
Lars Porsena perched on the limb above.
He called, "Caw, caw."
I did call William Shakespeare four times
and in between I called him by the bird call
that does mean I have needs of him.

He did come and he made a stop under the limb.
I was most glad.
My arms did have a queer feel from hanging there.
I was real glad just to sit quiet

on the back of William Shakespeare
while he did walk on.
And Lars Porsena did sit behind me.
We went on.

We had seeing of the section men
working on the railroad track.
They were making stoop-overs.
The men did wave their hands at us.
I did wave back.
I gave William Shakespeare two pats on the shoulder.
That means turn about.
He did.

We went in a slow way.
I did look looks about.
There were robins and bluebirds and larks.
When we was come to a bend in the road
I made a slide off William Shakespeare.
I went to pick him some grass.

A wagon went by.
Two horses were in front of it,
and on its high seat was a man
with his hat on sideways,
and a woman with a big fascinator
most hiding her face.
There was seven children in the wagon.
A little girl had a tam-o-shanter
and a frown and a cape on her.

I have thinks from the looks
on their faces they all did have wants
to get soon where they were going.
I smiled a smile and waved to the last
little girl of all on the wagon.
She smiled and waved her hand.

While we did have waiting
at the bend of the road,
the wind did say, "Je vien."
[*I am coming*]
The plants did answer make,
"Nous entendons."
[*We are waiting*]
Then the wind did say,
"Le printemps viendra bientot."
[*Spring will come soon*]
And the plants did answer,
"Nous fleurions bientot."
[*We will blossom soon*]
I did have glad feels.

When we were come again to a stump,
I did climb on again.
The light of the day
was going from blue to silver.
And thoughts had coming
down the road to meet us.
They were thoughts from out the mountains
where are the mines.

They were thoughts from the canyons.
I did feel their coming close about us.
Very near they were and all about.
We went very slow.
We had listens to the thoughts.
They were the soul thoughts
of little things that soon
will have their borning time.

It was coming near grey-light-time
and we could not have plain sees.
There were little fast patter sounds—
a horse riding down the road.
When he was most to where we were
the man did have the horse go in a slow way.
It was the man that wears grey neckties
and is kind to mice.
He did seem most glad that we
were on the road that he was on.
He did breathe satisfaction breathes
just like Sadie McKibben does
when she finds I haven't broken my bones
when I fall out of a tree.

Then he said, "The fairies left a note
in the moss box by the old log
for me to go and find you—
to bring you home again
before starlight-time."
And we were glad he was come,

for the stars were not
and dark was
before we were come home.

Jenny Strong is come to visit us.
She came on the logging train
in the morning of today.
She brought her bags with her.
The mama did send me to meet her
at the meeting of the roads.
The bags—they were heavy to carry,
and my arms got some tired.

As we did go along,
I did look looks at Jenny Strong.
The grey curls about her face
did have a proper look.
To get that proper look
she does them on curl papers.
I have seen her so do

when she was come to visit before.
And all her plumpness did most fill
the grey dress she was wearing.

The dress has little ruffles around the neck.
Her black bonnet has a pink rosebud on it,
and every time that Jenny Strong
does give her head a nod
that pink rosebud does give itself a nod.

When we were come to the gate,
Jenny Strong did hold her cape
and her grey dress up in a careful way.
She had blue stockings on
and they was fastened up with pink ribbons.
She went on while I did shut the gate.
I did come after.
I could not come after in a quick way
because the bags was heavy.

The way was dampness near the creek
and Jenny Strong did take dainty steps
as we did go along.
The pink rosebud did nod itself.
When we were come near unto the house,
there was a rooster by our front door.

After Jenny Strong took off her cape
and her black bonnet with the pink rosebud,
I did pull the best rocking chair out
in the middle of the room for her.

She sat in it while she did have talks with the mama.
I did go to teeter the baby on the bed
as the mama did say for me to do.

While she did talk,
Jenny Strong did rock big rocks.
One time she almost did rock over.
She breathed a big breath.
Then that she might not rock over again,
I did put a stick of wood under the rockers.
That helped some.
But, too, it did keep her from rocking.
She went on talking.

I went back to teeter the baby.
By and by the mama's baby did go to sleep,
and I made a start to go to my nursery.
Jenny Strong did ask me where I was going.
She said she thought she would like to go.
We went out the door.
Then I ran in a quick run back
to get her black bonnet with the pink rosebud.
I brought it to her.
She said, being as I did bring it to her
she would wear it,
but she had not in tent shuns to when we started.
I do so like to see that pink rosebud nod itself.

We went a little way down the path.
Jenny Strong did follow
over the little logs in a slow way.

I did make stops to help her.
The pink rosebud did nod.
When we were come to the nursery
I did show her the many baby seeds
I did gather by the wayside in the fall-time.
I did tell her how I was going
to plant them come spring-time.
She did nod her head.
The pink rosebud did nod.

After, I did show her the silk bags
with spider eggs in them.
Then I did show her all the cradles
the velvety caterpillars
did make at fall-time.
I did give her explainings how butterflies
and moths would be a-coming out of the cradles.
She gave her head some more nods.

I moved to where the woodmouse folks are.
I was going to show her what
a nice nose and little hands Mozart has.
When I did turn about to do so
there was Jenny Strong
going in funny little hops over the logs.
She was going in a hurry to the house.
I did have a wonder why.
Then I did sing a lullaby song
to all the woodmice in the nursery.

I did stop by some grand fir trees to pray.
When one does look looks up at the grand trees
growing up almost to the sky
one does always have longings to pray.

When I was come to the door
I heard the mama calling.
She did ask me what for was it I gave
Jenny Strong such a scare
and she did spank me most hard.

When I did go into the house
all the scares was gone off Jenny Strong.
Here I print.
She does sit in a rocking chair with her
feet propped up on a soapbox.
She hums as she sits.
She crochets as she hums.
She does make lace in a quick way,
but I have wonders about her.
She does not like mice.

Now Jenny Strong and the mama is gone
to the house of Elsie to see the new baby.
The mama did tell me to put the baby to sleep.
I so did.
I did sing it to sleep in the rocking chair.
I did sing:
"A is for Adour, Avre, Ain, Arroux."
When I did get to "D is for Douze and Dordogne

and Durance" the baby did move its arm.
When I did get to "G is for Garonne and Gers
and Gard" the baby did open its eyes.
When I did get to "I is for Indre and Isere
and Iraouaddy" it did close its eyes.
I did sing on.
And sleeps did come upon the baby.

We had lots on the table to eat tonight
because Jenny Strong is come.
And most everything I did get to eat
I did make divides of it for my friends.
There is enough for all to have a good amount
to eat, which often isn't.
The birds will like the scraps
that are on the plate of Jenny Strong,
if I can get them
before the mama gives them to the cat.

This day—it was a lonely day.
I did have longings all its hours
for Angel Mother and Angel Father.
Many times in the grey-light-time
I go on searches for the kisses of Angel Father.
The glad song in my heart is not bright today.
I have thinks as how
I can bring happiness to folks about.
That is such a help when lonesome feels do come.

Angel Mother did say,
"Make earth glad, little one—

that is the way to keep
the glad song ever in your heart.
It must not go out."

I do so try to keep it there.
I did have thinks as how I would stop
to get watercress for the mama
on the way home from school.
She does have such a fondness for it.
And too she does have longings
for singing lessons.
I am saving my pennies to buy her one.
All the pennies that the man that wears
grey neckties and is kind to mice
does give to me I save.
I have nineteen pennies.
And when I grow up I am going to buy her
a whole rain barrel of singing lessons.

Tomorrow I will be taking
Elizabeth Barrett Browning to visit
the girl who has no seeing.
They do both have likings for each other.
All my friends do have appreciations
of the pats she does give to them
and the words she does say.

She says when we are come,
"Here is come the kingdom of heaven."
I have feels she has mistakes about that
because the kingdom of heaven,

being up in the sky,
is there beyond the stars.

I tell her of the thoughts
growing with the trees and fleurs and leaves—
how they are God's thoughts
growing right up out of the earth.
Always she does ask for more.

When I did go my way
to the house we live in,
I put the watercress for the mama on the table.
No one was there.
Then I did bring much wood in
and put it in the woodbox.
After the chickens I went into the near woods.

I so went to tie messages I did print
on grey leaves to the trees.
I tied them there that they
may go in thoughts to Angel Mother
and Angel Father up in heaven.
When angels come to walk in the near woods
they will see and carry them on.
And every time I did tie on a leaf message
I did say a little prayer.

As I did walk along
I saw many grey rocks.
Some had grey and green patches on them.

Some patches had ruffles
all around their edges.
They are lichens.
My Angel Father did say so.
Lichen folk talk in grey tones.

I hear their voices more in December
than I do in June-time.
Angel Father did show me the way
to listen to lichen voices.
Most grownups don't hear them at all.
They walk right by—in a hurry sometimes.
And all the little lichen folks
are saying things.
I put my ear close to the rocks to listen.
They tell about the gladness
of the winter day.

The nipple on Elsie's baby bottle
has not stay ons.
It had come-offs a lot of times today.

Elsie did say, "I wish
it would stick tight this time."
I did tell her I had knows of a way
to make that nipple stick tight.
She said, "That's nice. I don't know of a way."

She had asks for me to show her.
I went back to the house we live in
to get the bottle of china mending glue.
I most fell off the stove, but I didn't.
That would have been a cal lamb of tea.

When I was come back to Elsie
she had askings what was she to do.
I told her to go in the bedroom
and shut her eyes while her wish came true.
She filled the baby's bottle with warm milk.
She went into the bedroom to wait waits.
A little time it took.
I had to have carefuls.
I made the glue in a nice ring around the top.
Then I put some more china-mending-glue-
guaranteed-to-stick in a ring
around the edge of the nipple.
That fixed it.

I put the china mending glue in my pocket.
When I did say, "It is fixed!"
Elsie did come.
She did have askings

how she was going to fix it
on the days I was not there.
I told her it wasn't me—
it was the china mending glue.

That was what did it.
She had a spell of a cough.
It came in a sudden way upon her
and tears came in her eyes.
Maybe her mother will have to come.
Whenever she has a cold
or feels of one a-coming
she does send in a quick way for her mother.
She told me thanks
for making her wish come true.

When I did give my dress a smooth-out
I had feels for the tear I got yesterday
on the barn door.
It was quite a big one.
I got a patch of flannel
that was almost like the dress.
I mended it on my dress with china mending glue.
It is quicker than mending it
with a needle and thread
in a regular way.

*T*he husband of Dear Love has given me
one of his old caps to carry my pets in.

Sometimes caterpillars do ride in it.
Sometimes Felix Mendelssohn and Mozart
do ride in it.
Today Brave Horatius did wear the cap.
He did bark a joy bark
and gave his tail three wags
and we did start to the house of Dear Love.

The husband of Dear Love
was making for her a chair.
He did make all little rough places
to have much smoothness.
He so did with tools out of a toolbox
he does keep in the kitchen.
When the toolbox has its lid down
it is a seat to sit on.

Sometimes on rainy days
I do take Thomas Chatterton Jupiter Zeus
to visit Dear Love
and we all sit on the toolbox.
He does allow Dear Love to give him
gentle pats on his nice white paws.

Today Dear Love did get a piece of
calico just like my dress.
Then she cut out the flannel patch
I did mend on with china mending glue.
She did sew on the calico in a nice way.
She thought the flannel would be nice

for a blanket for Felix Mendelssohn.
Her husband did smile and say,
"Another reason."

Now I have thinks the other reason was
the soft feels of the flannel
would get wored off and wouldn't be there
for the joy feels of Felix Mendelssohn.
He is a mouse that has likes for soft feels
to go to sleep in.

IV

*M*orning is glad on the hills.
The sky sings in blue tones.
Little blue fleurs are early blooming now.
I do so like blue.
It is glad everywhere.
When I grow up I am going to write a book
about the glad of blues.
The earth sings in green.

*W*illiam *Shakespeare* is having a rest day.
He is not working in the woods
with the other horses.
Tiredness was upon him.
I gave his nose rubs
and his neck and ears too.

And I did tell him poems
and sing him songs.
After I did sing more
sleeps come upon him.
While he was going to sleep
the breaths he did breathe
were such long breaths.
And I gave him more pats on the nose.
I'll come at supper time
so he may go in the barn
with the other horses.

I did.
Sleeps was still upon him.
I went to pet his front leg
but it was stiff.
I petted him on the nose—
but it was cold.
I called him but he did not answer.
I now go to tell the man who wears
grey neckties and is kind to mice
about his long sleep.

We are come back.
Now I do have understanding.
My dear William Shakespeare will
no more have wakeups again.
Rob Ryder cannot give him whippings no more.
He just had goes
because tired feels was upon him.

I have covered him over with leaves.
To find enough, I went to the far end
of the near woods.
I gathered them in my apron.
Sometimes I could hardly see my way
because I just could not keep from crying.
I have such lonesome feels.
I have thinks his soul
is not far gone away.
There are little blue fleurs
a-blooming where he did lay
him down to sleep.

*T*oday was wash day come again.
The mama had me empty the wash water.
There were two big tubs full of water.
That's an awful lot of water to empty.
But I carry it out in a sauce pan.
And sauce pans of water are not so heavy.

Then the mama did have me to weed onions.
My back did get some tired feels

but the onions were saying,
"We thank you for more room to grow."

I went to see the new baby of Elsie.
It was sleeping in the cradle
that the husband of Elsie did make from a box.
He put rockers on the box
and Elsie put soft feels in it.
And while she sews Elsie does rock
the cradle with her foot.
She sings, "Rock-a-bye baby in the tree top.
When the wind blows the cradle will rock."
I did stay quite a long time
to look upon the face of the baby.
I do so love babies.

Every night I pray for twins
I want when I grow up.
Some nights I pray they may have
blue eyes and golden hair.
Other nights I pray for them
to have brown eyes and brown hair.
Sadie McKibben says I better stop
changing my prayers so much
or the angels may bring to me twins
with streaked hair and variegated eyes.

When I was come to the house of Sadie McKibben
she was washing clothes.

On wash days Sadie McKibben
does look a bit different.
Her hair does hang in strings about her face.
Her dress does have crinkles all adown it.
Her nice blue gingham apron
does have rumples and soapy smells
when I cuddle close to her on wash days.

Today I did go to weed her onions for her.
They did have looks like they have needs
for more room to grow in.

*W*e did christen Solomon Grundy.
He is such a dear baby pig.
He was borned a week ago on Monday.
And this being Tuesday, we did christen him for
the rhyme the grandpa does sing about
Solomon Grundy being christened on Tuesday.

I made him a christening robe
out of a new dish towel
but the aunt had no appreciations
of the great need
for a christening robe.
My ears were slapped until I thought
my head would pop open,
but it didn't.
It just ached.
Last night when I went to bed
I prayed for the ache to go away.

This morning when I woke up
it had gone out the window.
I did feel good feels
from my head to my toes.

I thought about the christening.
I crawled on my hands and knees
back under the shed where he
and his five sisters and his little brother
were all having breakfast from their mother.
I gently did pull away his hind legs
from among all those dear baby pigs.
He has the most curl in his tail.

I took him to the pump
and pumped water on him
to get every speck of dirt off.
He squealed because the water was cold.
So I took some of the mama's warm
wash water and did give him a warm bath.
Then he was the pinkest white pig you ever saw.
I took the baby's talcum powder can
and sprinkled him all over.
He did give a squeal.
Then I climbed right out the bedroom
window because the mama was coming fast.

A little ways we did go and I did ask
that grand fir tree, Good King Edward I,
to be his godfather.

After the naming of him,
I did say the Lord's prayer softly
over the head of Solomon Grundy.
After I said Amen, I did poke him
in among all his sisters
and near unto his mother.
Aphrodite gave a grunt of satisfaction.
Also did Solomon Grundy.

I went to the house.
The little girl was romping on the bed.
I helped her get her clothes on.
Then we went to the kitchen for breakfast.
The mama told me to get the mush
for the little girl's breakfast.
I spooned it out into a blue dish
that came as premium in the box of mush.

Then I went to tend the chickens.
I carried feed to them.
I counted all the chickens that were there.
There weren't as many as there ought to be.
Some hens were setting in the chicken house.
I went in.
I lifted them off.
I did carry them out to the feed.
They were fidgety and fluffy and clucky.

While they were eating their breakfast
I counted their eggs.
Minerva hadn't as many as the others.

I took an egg from each nest and
put it into the nest of Minerva.

Then I thought I would go explores,
but the mama called me to
scour the pots and pans.
That is something
I do not like to do at all.
So all the time I'm scouring
I keep saying lovely verses.
That helps so much.
And by and by the pots and pans are clean.

After that—all day—the mama did have
more works for me to do.
There was more wood to bring in.
There was steps to scrub.
There was cream to be shaked into butter.
There was raking to do in the yard.
There was carpet strings to sew together.
In between times there was the baby to tend.
And all day long I did have longings
to go on exploration trips.
The most hurry time of all was eventime
for company was coming to eat at the table.

I came here to the barn.
I sit here printing.
In between times I stretch out on the hay.
I feel tired and sore all over.
I have tried so hard to help her today.

Solomon Grundy is grunting here beside me.
I showed him the books
from Angel Mother and Angel Father.
They are such a comfort.
Angel Mother and Angel Father do seem nearer.
I did bow my head and ask my guardian angel
to tell them there in heaven
about Solomon Grundy being christened today.
Then I drew him up closer to my apron
and I patted him often.
And some of the pats I gave him
were for the lovely Peter Paul Rubens
that used to be.
The more pats I gave Solomon Grundy
the closer he snuggled up beside me.
I will sing him a lullaby
before I take him back to his mother.

*T*oday I went to visit Dear Love
with Solomon Grundy in one arm
and Thomas Chatterton Jupiter Zeus in the other.
Solomon Grundy wore his christening robe
and he looked very sweet in it.
I gave him a nice warm bath before we did start,

so as to get all the pig pen smell off.
Sometimes smells do get in that pig pen
though I do give it brush outs every day,
and I do carry old leaves and bracken fern
and straws for beds for Aphrodite.

As we did go along I did sing.
Then I did tell about the beautiful love
the man of the long step that whistles
most of the time does have for the penseé
girl with the faraway look in her eyes.
Sadie McKibben says he picks bunches of flowers
in the woods for her.
Then he does lay them down because
he is afraid to take them to her.
Sadie McKibben says he is a very shy man.

Solomon Grundy did grunt a little grunt.
So I did sing to him:
"Did He smile His works to see?
Did He who made the lamb make thee?"
He grunted a grunt with a question in it.
"Indeed He did, Solomon Grundy, indeed He did.
And the hairs of thy baby head—they are numbered."

When we were come to the house of Dear Love
her husband was making a flower bed
for Dear Love to plant morning glory seeds in.
Then morning glory vines
will grow up around the window.
I think that will be nice.

I sat down beside her.
She had on her blue gingham apron
with cross stitches on it.
I did count thirty cross stitches.
Some day I will count them all.

*T*hen we went to the woods.
On the path that goes to the moss box
I did see flowers on the ground.
They was the flowers that the man of the
long step that whistles most all of the time
did gather for the penseé girl with the
faraway look in her eyes.
Some of the flowers was all faded.

I put some moss in my basket
that I do carry baby chickens in.
Then I did put in some of the flowers.
I put in the most faded ones
because they had been waiting waits the longest.
Then we all did hurry to the house
of the aunt of the penseé girl.

The aunt was not there
and we were glad.
But the penseé girl with the faraway look
in her eyes was there.
She came to the door when
we did tap upon its handle.

I did tell her all in one breath
that we was bringing the flowers
that the man with the long step
that whistles most of the time
did gather for her on many days.
And she did take them up in her arms.

And I told her my dog's name
was Brave Horatius
and he was a fine dog,
and that Thomas Chatterton Jupiter Zeus
was a most lovely woodrat,
and I held out his white paw
for her to have feels of,
but he did pull it back
and cuddle close to me.
I told her how he was shy too
and when he had knows of her better
he would let her pat his nice white paws.

Then I did hurry back to bring her
the rest of the flowers.
And she was glad for them.
She did go back with us to the log
where the flowers was
and there was joy-lights in her eyes.
When we did go along I did tell her
about the great love the man of the long step
that whistles most all of the time
does have for her.

Quietness was upon her
and we did walk in a slow way.
She did kneel down by them for a long time
and look at all the bunches of flowers.
I saw a chipmunk
and did follow after
to see where his home was.

*T*oday I didn't get to finish
the exploration trip over the river
because after I did my morning work
the mama grabbed me.
She did tie me to the woodshed corner
with a piece of clothesline.
So we couldn't go explores together
she did tie the very wise crow, Lars Porsena,
to another corner.
She said if I was her born child
I wouldn't have this longing
to go on exploration trips.

The day was growing warm.
When it grew awful hot
my arms did have feelings too sore
to lean over any more to see Lars Porsena.
I sat down and did watch the passers-by.
There was the Rhode Island red rooster
and the Plymouth Rock hen.
Then a butterfly did rest

on the handle of the well pump
where I did have longings to be.

The wee mother hummingbird never left her nest.
I could see her bill.
I did have hopes Brave Horatius would come by.
I called and I did hear his whine afar off.
Then I new he was tied up too.

The old black cat sat on the doorstep.
He had a saucer of milk
and he did wash his face.
I would have been partly glad
if he did come over to see me.
I haven't made up with him
since he did catch the baby robin.

A grasshopper came hopping along.
I stuck out my foot and he did hop over it.
I was having very sad feels.
The sun got hotter and hotter.
And pretty soon I did have
queer feels in the head
and then my nose did begin to bleed.
I felt all choked up and sticky.
And every time I gave my head a shake
to get a good breath,
my curls did get mixed up
with the nose bleed.

Pretty soon the mama did see
my apron with blood upon it.
She untied me.

After she did souse me in the tub
under the pump I felt better.
My arms did tingle
where the rope was tied.
When the wood was all stacked up
the mama did say I might
take the ducklings to the brook.
That did make me very happy.
All the way to the brook I did sing
"Sanctus, sanctus, Dominus Deus."

*N*ow is the borning-time of year.
I did hurry home from school
in a quick way this afternoon.
The shepherd boy, Aidan of Iona
come from Lindisfarne,
has said I may name the little lambs
that are coming.

All day I did have thinks
of names to call them by.
I could hardly wait waits
till school-getting-out-time.
I had remembers how Sadie McKibben
says no child should grow a day old

without having a name.
Now some of those dear baby lambs
are two and three days
since their borning-time.

When I was come to the shepherd
I did tell him
now I have come to name all your lambs.
He did have one little lamb in his arms.
He did tell me as how
it didn't belong to anyone
and it was lonesome without a mother.
He said he would give it to me to mother.

I was so happy.
It was very white and very soft
and its legs was slim
and it had wants for a mother.
It had likes for me to put my arms around it.
I did name it first of all.
I called it Euripides.
It had likes for the taste of my fingers
when I did dip them into the pan of milk
and put them in its mouth.
Its wooly tail did wiggle joy wiggles.
I felt such a big amount
of satisfaction feels—
having a lamb to mother.
I am getting quite a big family now.

I was going to get a bottle
for my little lamb,
but Aidan of Iona come from Lindisfarne
did say that Euripides was full up
of milk for today and I could bring
his bottle on the morrow.

Then I did make begins
to name the other lambs.
They were dear and so dear.
First one I did come to I did name Plutarch.
The next one I did name Marcus Aurelius.
One was more big than the others.
I named him Homer.
He gave his tail a wiggle
and came close to his mother.

The shepherd did have likes for the names.
I did tell him how I have likes for them too.
After I said goodbye to all the other lambs
I did kiss Euripides on the nose.
Maybe he does have longs for kisses
like the longs I do have
for them every night-time.

*T*hen I did go to have sees of a cream lily
that has its growing
near unto the cathedral.
I have watched the leafing of that lily
and I have watched its budding.

A long time I have had thinks about it.
Today its blooming-time was come.
There it was.

I went close unto it.
My soul was full of thank feels.
Ever since the day when Peter Paul Rubens
did go away I have looked for his soul.
Now I have knows his soul
does love to linger by this lily.
I did kneel by it and say a thank prayer
for the blooming of this fleur.
If ever I go from here
I will take with me this lily plant.
I did have feels
that my dear Peter Paul Rubens
was very near this eventime.

I went to see Minerva in the hen house.
I saw her feathers were more fluffy
and there was some more heads
than hers in the nest.
There was the heads of the little chickens
I did pick out names for
before they was yet hatched.
And now I cannot tell them apart.

Minerva had one baby four days ago
and one baby three days ago
and soon she will have fifteen children.

I told her the names
I did pick for her children.
There is Edmund Spenser and John Fletcher
and Sir Francis Bacon and Oliver Goldsmith.
And when I did tell her
she ate all the grain in my hand.
It is so nice she has so many children.
I do so like to pick out names.

Now there is need for me to get those
christening robes done for her children.
On the day of their christening
I will carry them in a little basket
to the cathedral.
They are very delicate.
Today I did show Minerva the little cap
with ruffles on it that I have just made
for her to wear at their christening.
I made it like Jenny Strong's morning cap.
When I told Minerva she did chuckle
some more chuckles.

Today I went not to school.
The mama did have me cut potatoes into pieces.
Tonight and tomorrow night the grownups
will plant the pieces of potatoes.
After, the ones with eyes on them
will have baby potatoes under the ground.
Up above the ground
they will be growing leaves and flowers.

One must leave an eye
on every piece of potato one plants.
It won't grow if you don't.
It can't see how to grow
without its eye.

All day today I did be careful
to leave an eye on every piece.
And I did have meditations about what things
the eyes of potatoes
do see there in the ground.
I have thinks they do have seeing
of black velvet moles
and large earthworms.
I have longings for more eyes.
There is much to see
in this world all about.

*T*oday was dyeing day.
The mama dyed old clothes.
First she washed them in the tub.
Then she put them in the boiler on the stove.
In the boiler was beautiful blue water.

She made this water blue with little specks
that came out of an envelope
in a quick hurry.
And when she took them out
all the clothes was blue.
And after they hung on the line
they was yet blue
and I see them quiver blue quivers
when the wind blows.

The mama did leave the boiler
of blue water on the stove.
She is gone to the house of her mother.
She told me to watch the house
and not let the fire go out.
It is a long time
and the boiler has cold feels.
I stood upon the stove
and put my finger in it.

I have been keeping watches
of the house like she did say.
And in between I have been
reading the books that Angel Mother
and Angel Father did write in.
Now I am going to have dyeing day
like the mama did have.
It is so much fun to lift things
up and down in blue water.

First I did dye the mama's clothespin bag.
It was brownness before.
I took all the clothespins out first.
Then I did give them all a dip.
They did bob about in a funny way.
I made whirls in the blue water with my fingers.

Then I made a start to dye handles.
First I dipped in the butcher knife handle.
Then I did give the dipper handle a dip
and the hammer handle.

Minerva came to the back porch.
I had thinks she might have
likes for blue feathers.
So I did give her a gentle dip.
She walked right out our door
without even a thank chuckle.

I had seeing of a box of matches
so I did give it a dip.
It has a limp feel.
And all the matches now are blue.
I laid them in rows on the grass to dry.

*A*fter morning work was done
I took my little basket
full of christening robes
to the hen house where Minerva is.

One baby chicken didn't hatch.
Yesterday Elsie did help me
to make christening robes.
She put a little ruffle of lace on one.

I thought they did have needs
of little bows.
Elsie said she had thinks that way too.
In her sewing basket she did find some ribbons.
She tied them all into little bows.
There was enough for every baby chicken.
And I did sew them on at night-time
at the house of the mama.

The chickens waited waits
in the corner of the basket
while I did put the christening
robes on the others.
Oliver Goldsmith had a little pink bow on his.
He would not keep still while I was
getting him into his robe.
He peeped three times.

Sir Francis Bacon did wear the christening
robe with the ruffle of lace around it,
and before I did get him put back in the basket
he did catch his toe in that ruffle of lace.
Then he peeped.
I took his toe out of the ruffle.

After I did get little brown John Fletcher
and all the rest of the children
into their robes
then I did take out of my pocket
the little white cap
with the ruffles on it.
I tied it under Minerva's bill.
She was a sweet picture in it
coming down the cathedral aisle by my side.
It is not often that Minerva talks,
but she did chuckle all the time
while her babies were being christened.

I did sing softly a hymn to the morning.
Then I did sing "Hosanna in Excelsis"
and took them all back to their house.
After, I did give Minerva
some goodbye pats and advices
about bringing up her children.

*A*fter morning works were done
I put some milk in the bottle for Euripides.
He was waiting waits for me by the pasture bars.
He is a most wooly lamb
and he was glad for his breakfast.

The other lambs did make jumps about.
Their ways are ways of playfulness.
While I was looking looks at them

Euripides did some way
get the nipple off his bottle,
and the rest of the milk
did spill itself out.
I hid the bottle by a rock.

Euripides did follow after me.
He does follow me manywheres I do go.
I looked for fleurs that I had longs to see.
I lay my ear close to the ground
where the grasses grew close together.
I did listen.
There were voices from out the earth
and the things of their saying
were the gladness of growing.
And there was music.
And in the music there was sky-twinkles
and earth-twinkles.
All the grasses growing there
did feel glad feels
from the tips of their green arms
to their toe roots in the ground.

Brave Horatius and the rest of us
didn't get home until after supper-time.
The folks was gone.
I found some supper for him
and put it in his special dish.
Then I came in to get some bread and milk.
There was rumblings of distress
come from the backyard.

I looked out the window.
There near the dog's special dish
sat Lars Porsena with a strange forlorn look.
Brave Horatius had pulled out
all the tail feathers of the crow.

I felt disturbs.
I had not knowings what to do for it.
First I put some mentholatum on a bandage.
Then I did wrap it around Lars Porsena
from back to front,
in under his wings.
and twice on top so the bandage
would stay in place
where his tail feathers did come out.

Then I did start to the hospital.
I only did have going a little way
when I did meet the man that wears
grey neckties and is kind to mice.
He did have askings about my crow.
I told him explanations.
He pondered on the matter.
Then he picked me and Lars Porsena up
and set us down on a stump.
He told me there was no needs
for me to have wonders
about how long before
new tail feathers do come.
He said birds do lose their tail feathers
and do grow them on again.

Then he did take up Lars Porsena in his arms.
He unwrapped all the bandages.
When they was off
Lars Porsena did give himself a stretch
and his wings a little shake.
And I said a little prayer
for his getting a new tail soon.
And the man that wears grey neckties
and is kind to mice said Amen.

Men are such a comfort—
men that wear grey neckties
and are kind to mice.
He does love the grand fir trees
that do grow in the forest.
I have seen him stretch out his arms to them
just like I do in the cathedral.

*B*en Jonson pecked Sir Francis Bacon on the head.
I said prayers over them
for peace between them.
Then I put one in a little box
on a log and the other one
in a little box on another log.

The boxes was alike.
Today I had sees of those two
drinking out of the water pan together.
Peace was between them.

*T*oday we all did go for a walk.
With my right hand I did lead
the girl who has no seeing.
As we did go along we did have listens
to the voices of the trees and grass.
She is learning what the grasses say.
Too, she is learning to see things.
She shuts her eyes when I shut mine.
We go on journeys together.
We ride in a cloud—
in a fleecy white one
that does sail away over the hills.

The girl who has no seeing
asks when I am going to bring
Euripides to visit her.
She said she thinks
he must be a big lamb now that I give him
his bottle every morning and eventime.
I said he is a very dear lamb.

Then she had asking when Thomas Chatterton
Jupiter Zeus and Virgil was coming to visit her.
And she had wants for Lars Porsena to come.
I did tell her we would all come
to visit her on the fourth day
from the day that is now.

*E*very day Aphrodite does have likes
for her feeding trough to be scrubbed
clean all over.
And I have planted fern and fleurs
all around her pig pen.

After I did get moss and cover the feed trough
it was a good place to sit
and draw a picture of Solomon Grundy.
I drew his portrait by his mother's side.
Then I had him stand on his feet
and I drew one of him that way.

It was almost done.
There was a little noise.
I went on drawing Solomon Grundy's ears
and his curly tail.
Then I had knows what it was.
The chore boy came to feed the pigs—
and he poured all that bucket of swill
on top the moss
and Solomon Grundy's portrait

and me.
The feels I did feel—they was drippy ones.
Then I did go in a quick way to the creek
to get the swill-smells off.
First I did wade out a little way.
Then I sat down.
The water came up to my neck.
I gave my hair a wash-off.
By and by I did have feels
that I was clean again.

At the house I did give my clothes
some wringouts by the steps
so the water would not have drips
on the kitchen floor.
The mama was at Elsie's house.
When I did have dry clothes on
I did hang the wet ones on some bushes
in the woods to dry.
And while I did so
I saw a mother bird and father bird
in their comings and goings to a nest.
Now are busy times.

I did go to the folks in the nursery.
A little way into the woods
I saw a man coming.
He did take long steps.
When he was come nearer I had seeing

it was the man that wears grey neckties
and is kind to mice.

I did hide behind a tree.
He came on.
When he was near the tree he did say,
"I thought I saw someone coming.
Guess I was mistaken.
I think I'll take these splints
for the hospital back to the mill."

When I did hear him say that
I ran in a quick way out.
He was looking long looks away.
Then I did give his coat sleeve a pull
and he did whistle,
he was so surprised.

Then he did go with me to the hospital
and while I did hold little Sir Francis Bacon,
the man that wears grey neckties
and is kind to mice did fix the splints
on his hurt leg in a gentle way.
He did have his leg hurt in a real bad way
and the folks was going to kill him,
but they gave him to me for my very own
because a chicken isn't any good
with a broke leg.

Now is the fourth day.
First I did make begins
to get my family all together.
Brave Horatius was waiting by the back steps.
Lars Porsena was near unto him.
His appears are not what they were before.
I am praying for a tail real soon.
Virgil was under the front step.
I did squeak calls for Thomas Chatterton
Jupiter Zeus to come out of his house.
He did come out
and he did crawl upon my shoulder.

We made a start.
We went to the nursery to get Mozart.
We went to the pasture to get Euripides.
He's a very jumpy lamb.
He did jump a long jump to meet us today
and his tail did wiggle more wiggles.
We went down the lane.

We made a stop to get Solomon Grundy.
We went out along the road.
They were a sweet picture.
I made a stop to look at them all—
some running ahead and some behind.
And they all did have joy feels
that they were going
to the girl who has no seeing.

I did feel a big amount of satisfaction
that I have such a nice family.

We all did walk right up to the door.
We had knows only she would be there
because this is the going-to-town-day
of her people.
I knocked more knocks.
Solomon Grundy squealed his most nice
baby pig squeal.
We did listen listens.
She had not comings to the door.
While we had waits I did sing to them.
I had wonders why she did not come.

After a while I did go sit
on the gatepost to wait waits.
It was a long time.
A man on a horse went by.
He had asks what for I was sitting on that post.
I did tell him I was waiting waits
for the coming of the girl
with no seeing.
He did look off to the hills.
Then he started to say something
but he swallowed it.
He looked off to the hills again.
Then he did say,
"Child, she won't come back."

I did smile a sorry smile upon him
because I had knows he didn't know her.
It is not often she goes anywhere,
but when she does she does always come back.
I waited more waits.
Then it was time for us to all get home.
I will go goes again tomorrow
to see the girl that has no seeing,
for I have knows she will come again home
tonight in starlight-time.

Yesterday the coffee pot tipped over on Harold.
He had pains—worse than when
the baby has colic.
Elsie put oil on him.
When she put oil on him
we did not hear his cries anymore.
I feel I have needs
of that oil in my hospital.

I sat down on a log to pick out names
for the twins I am going to have

when I grow up.
I picked out a goodly number of names
but I could not have decides.
I had thinks I would wait a little time.

*E*arly on this morning I went again
to the house of the girl who has no seeing.
There were little singings everywhere.
I cuddled Thomas Chatterton
Jupiter Zeus in my arms.
He is a most dear velvety woodrat.
I tiptoed on the grass.
Euripides did make little jumps beside me.
And Brave Horatius came a-following after.

I made a stop by the window
and rapped six raps.
Six raps means Come On Out—We Are Come.
I had no hears of her steps a-coming
like they always do.
I put my hands above my eyes
so I could see inside the window.
She was not there.
Nobody was.
I did six raps again.
She did not come.

I crawled around by the lilac bush.
I waited waits for her coming.

Two men were talking by the fence.
One did say, "It is better so."
The other man did say, "A pit tea it was
she couldn't have a little sight
to see the brush fire ahead."

And I had hears of the other one say,
"Probably the smell of the smoke caused
her to worry about the fire coming to the house,
and she was trying to find out where it was
when she walked right into it."
And the other man did ask
if she was con chus after.
And the other one did say, "Yes."

I had wonders what did it all mean.
Another man did come to the gate.
He was the man who did come yesterday.
I felt queerness in my throat.
I didn't see either.

More the men said.
All her clothes did have fire
and then she ran
and her running
did make the fire to burn her more—
and she stubbed her toe and fell.
She fell in a place
where there was mud and water.
She was rolling in it when they found her.

And all the fire-pains did make her moan
moans until hours after when she died.
And I couldn't see anything by then.

When I did walk away
I did have sees of the little fleurs
along the way that she so did love.
I have thinks they were having longings
for her presence. And I was too.
Her soul will come again to the woods.
And she will have sees for the blooming
of the flowers that she has loves for.
I go now to write a message
on a leaf for her
like I do to Angel Mother
and Angel Father.
The angels will carry it
up to her in heaven.

*B*ecause Aphrodite cannot get out of her pig pen,
I did have decides to have cathedral service there.
Brave Horatius came in.
Thomas Chatterton Jupiter Zeus
nestled by my side.
Solomon Grundy lay by his mother.
Felix Mendelssohn did snuggle
in my apron pocket.
And in the other pocket was Virgil.

After some long time,
when all was settled down to quietness,
I did start the service.
It took a long time to get quietness
because the dear folks weren't used to
having service in the pig pen.

I did start:
"I will lift mine eyes up unto the hills."
I lifted most all the congregation up
to have a peek.
I did lift them up one at a time.
And so they saw and lifted up their eyes
unto the hills.
But most of them didn't.
They looked in different ways.
Thomas Chatterton Jupiter Zeus
did not have seeing for more
than the piece of cheese
I hid in my sleeve for him.
He gave his cheese squeaks.
I gave him a nibble.

When I did finish prayers
Brave Horatius did bark Amen.
I gave him a pat and then did say,
"Blessed be the pure in heart,
for they shall see God."

V

*R*ain is come some more.
It came all night.
The earth is damp again and things grow more.
Some things grow very fast. Weeds do.

The mama had me hoe between the rows
of things that do grow in the garden.
I wonder if I would get roots
if I planted my feet some inches in the soil
and did keep still a long time.
Some day I'll try it and find out.

The earthworms are out again.
I wonder how it feels to stretch out long
and then get short again.

By and by I saw another earthworm.
He was alone.

Virgil did have seeing too.
He did walk walks around that earthworm.
Then he did take it in a quick way.
It was very big.
Toads do have such useful hands.
He did have needs to use his
to stuff it down his throat.
The earthworm made wiggles.
And Virgil gave it pushes down his throat.

*I*n the afternoon-time I did have talks
with Michael Raphael about the girl
who has no seeing.
Then I did go to play on the hay.
I had hearings of a sound in the stall below.
I slid a slide down into the manger.

There was someone I have never had sees of before.
He has big eyes and a velvet nose
and he is brownish.

When I did land there
he did have afraid looks.
But I just sat quiet in the corner
and reached handfuls of hay to him.
He is that new sorrel horse
I heard the grandpa say he was going to get.
And now he is got.
I have likes for him.
I told him a poem.

I did tell him that his name is Savonarola.
And all the time the raindrops
did make little joy patters on the roof.

When I was coming back from the house of Elsie
I saw a piece of bark.
I did turn it over with care.
There were ants.
I sat down to watch them.
Some ants did carry bundles with queer looks.
Big Jud at school says they are ant eggs.
But I have not thinks so.
I remember Angel Father did call them
nymphes de fourmis.

Today Lars Porsena did walk
on the clean tablecloth.
It looked most queer
to see a crow on a table inside.
He was tracking crow tracks
in jam all over it.
I picked him up
and the mama picked me up
and right away she did spank me
for his doing it.
The time it did take to wash
that tablecloth was a long time.
I made little rubs where the jam tracks were.
When they was all out

the mama did tell us
to get out of her way.
We did.

We went to the house of Sadie McKibben.
She has a new back comb.
I put it in her hair for the first time.
It has crinkles and does hold her hair
up from her neck in a nice way.

Sometimes Sadie McKibben lets me do her hair.
I do roll it in a roll on top her head.
It makes loop looks where some hairs
want not to be in the roll.
Then I put hairpins in
to make them look like a waterwheel.
Her hair does not stay up long.

Today she smiled and did give me a kiss
on both my cheeks and one on my nose.
I have glad feels that she does
remember about the nose.

Very early in the morning of today
I did get out of my bed
and dress in a quick way.
The sun was up and the birds were singing.
The mama did tell me works to do
and then she went with the little girl

and the baby
and some lace she was making for a baby shirt
all to the house of Elsie.
I did make begins on the works.
When all was finished I made prepares
for Thomas Chatterton Jupiter Zeus
to visit Dear Love.
It is four whole days
since she has seen him.

I put on his nice pink ribbon
that the fairies did bring him.
Then I did wash his beautiful white paws.
I dried them on the little towel
that Dear Love made for him.
It is like her big bath towel.
She marked his initials on it with red ink.
She put a dot after each letter.
T. C. J. Z. on his bath towel.

Dear Love was so glad to see us.
I did tell her how I was praying every day
for her baby to come real soon.
And we did see a chipmunk.
We had a very nice visit.

When I was coming my way home
I saw the honeysuckles.
I nod to them as I go by.
They talk in shadows

with the little people of the sun.
And this I have learned—
grownups do not know the language of shadows.
Angel Mother and Angel Father did know
and they taught me.
I do so want them.
Sometimes they do seem near.
I have thinks sometimes kind God
just opens up the gates of heaven
and lets them come out to be
guardian angels for a little while.

When I did eat my bowl of bread and milk
I did have thinks I would make portraits
on the four white poker chips.
One is for Elizabeth Barrett Browning.

I will have to draw her head in a small way
so the horns can get in the picture too.
The people who make poker chips
ought to make them with more bigness.

Already in the hollow log,
where I do go on rainy days,
I have a goodly number of poker chip
portraits of my family.
One of the logging men at the mill
said he will give me more.

The chore boy does have objects
to my drawing on his poker chips.
He hides them in the barn.
I had not knows what they were
when I first found them.
I did make portraits of Michael Raphael
and Virgil and Lars Porsena.
The next day the chore boy
did give my curls a pull.
"What for did you mark up
my nice poker chips with your old pictures?"
Then I did have knows
they were his poker chips.

I did tell him that the white ones
had wants to have portraits on them.
He said he had more knows
what poker chips want than I have thinks.
He says poker chips want to be on a table
in a game with men.
He has not knows what he is talking about.

Then I did have a little longing
to rock again the baby's cradle.
Elsie was stirring things together
in a quick way
in the most big yellow bowl.
She was making for her young husband
a whipped cream cake.
He has such a fondness for them.

And she does make them for him
as often as there is cream enough.

While she did so
the baby did have a wake-up.
She let me give its cradle little touches
on its corner with my fingers
so to rock it in a gentle way.

In the morning of today was churning work.
While I did make the handle
with cross sticks go up and down
I did have hearings of the flowers in the field.
When butter was come
the mama did take it out the churn.
She put all the little yellow lumps
in a wood bowl.
Then she gave them pats and more pats.
When butter was its proper form
the mama did throw the butter paddle
across the table.

She said she hoped she would never
see that paddle again.
She won't.
I floated it away on the creek.

*L*ola has got her white silk dress
that she did have so much wants for.
It has a little ruffle around the neck
and one around each sleeve like she did say.
She said she would stand up
and stretch out her arms and bestow her blessing
on all the children like the deacon does—
but she didn't.
She didn't even raise up her hands.
She stayed asleep in that long box
the whole time the children
was marching around her
and singing "Nearer My God to Thee."
She did just lay there
with her white silk dress on
and her eyes shut
and her hands folded
and she was very still all the time.

Her sister did cry.
I did walk up to her and touch her hand
where she did sit in the rocking chair
in her house.
I did ask if it was a white silk dress

she was having wants for too.
She patted my hand.
I told her how nice it was
Lola did have hers, what she had wants for.
And Lola's sister did pat me on the head
and went out to her kitchen.

*A*mong the grasses on a little bush
there was a katydid.
Its green was a pretty greenness.
Its wings, they were folded close.
And it was washing its front feet.
Katydids do keep their feet most clean.
They do wash them again and more times.
I so do like to keep watches
of the way the katydid does clean its face
with its front foot.

When I was come to the little pond
I lay myself down close to its edge.
There were sky-clouds in the water.
I saw minnows all about.
First they were still.
Then they made moves about.
I saw a little cradle of tiny stones.
It was about an inch long.
While I did look looks at it,
it walked off.

Solomon Grundy was coming after me.
His little legs did bring him a quick way.
I made a stop to wait for him.
He was joys all over.
He did jump upon me.
And his squeals were squeals of gladness.
We went on together.

When we were come to the house of Dear Love
they were standing by the steps.
The husband of Dear Love
did bring home to her
a little nest that was in a tree
they did cut down today.
The baby birds were most ready to fly
when the tree did fall.
All six little birds but one
did get death as the tree fell.
They were such little things
when we did take them out.

The one live one was hungry.
We did feed him little bits at a time
from the egg that was left
in the dinner pail of the husband of Dear Love.
It did give to this little bird
some satisfaction feels.
Dear Love did cuddle it warm in her hands,
and her husband did make the egg

into little divides for me to give to it.
It did open its mouth most wide.

When I so did see it do,
I did open my mouth too like it did.
The husband of Dear Love did laugh.
I did have asking of him why he did laugh,
for it was not thoughtful to laugh
at a little hungry bird that did have
so hungry feels and lonesome ones.
He did say in his gentle way
that it was not at the little bird
he did laugh.
He laughs sometimes when he has thinks
about things at work.

I told him it was nice that he
had thoughtfuls of the nest.
He said he thought of me
and that made him think it would be nice
to bring the nest home.
And every time I did drop a piece of egg
into the mouth of the little bird,
I did open my mouth wide too
from seeing the bird do it.

When it was full of satisfaction feels,
Dear Love did fix it all up nice
in a warm little box.
She is going to give it careful cares

so it will grow up.
She has asked me to pick out a name for it.
I am so going to do.
And tomorrow I am going to have a funeral
of the other five birds that did get death
as the tree did fall.

Dear Love gave me white soft pieces
to wrap them in
and the husband of Dear Love
says he will make the tombstones
for the graves.
I am going to bury them
at a place in my forest
I call Dreux by Blaise.
There they will rest.
On tomorrow it so will be.

*T*oday I saw a yellow butterfly
near a mud puddle.
She came. She went.
Every time she did come
she did take a bit of mud.
I did watch.
When she was gone away
a little hole was where she did take mud.
She did make comes again.
It was for mud she did come every time.
Last time I did follow after.

She was so little a person
and the way she did go—
it was a quick way.
And I had seeing she was making
a cradle of mud for a baby guepe to be.

*W*hen morning works was done
I did put on my sunbonnet
to call on the rabbits
who live near the garden.
They are sunbonnet folks.
There was Madame Lapine.
She is a gentle woman
and her ways are quiet ways
and she does have fondness for cabbage.
I have showed her the way into the garden
when I am not there to get it for her.

Then I saw the chore boy near the barn.
He had a long stick.
He was knocking down the homes
of the swallows.
There were broken cradles on the ground.
There were grownup swallows
with distresses in their flying.
I did tell him how dear swallows are,
but he would have no listens.

When I did go goes
to the house of Sadie McKibben.
She was having troubles.
Just when she did have all her clothes
hung out to dry—
then the clothesline did break
and they all had falls on the ground.
While she did gather them up
she did have talks with herself.

She did say, " 'Tis a folly to fret—
grief's no comfort."
When her bread gets burns in the oven,
and the chickens bother on the porch,
and the clothes boil over on the stove,
and everything seems to go wrong,
Sadie McKibben has a way of saying,
" 'Tis a folly to fret—grief's no comfort."

While she was giving more wash-outs
to them clothes that did fall,
she did sing.
She sings on days when sunshine is.
She sings on days when rain is.
Sadie McKibben always sings
before the summer rain as does the robin.

When she did have them clothes
part hung on the line to dry again,

then did come by the man that wears
grey neckties and is kind to mice.
He was on his way to the mill town.
He had asks if there was anythings
she was having needs of
that he could bring back.
And she did say "bacon" and "some soda"
and some more things.
While she told him
he did write it down.

I breathed a big breath
when I did see his writing.
I said, "Oh."
He did turn himself around.
"What is it, little one?"
And I did tell him all in one breath.
"Oh, it's that you write in the way
the fairies write that do put notes
for me in the moss box where the old log is."
Then he did smile a slow smile.
When he did start to go
I heard him say to Sadie McKibben
"I guess I will have to change my writing."

When he did tell me goodbye, I did say,
"Please don't change your writing
because you write the way the fairies do.
I think the way they write is lovely."

Then he did say he guessed
it would be pretty hard—
trying to write another way
from what the fairies did teach him.
It is a very beautiful way.
Some of the letters are like
ripples on the water.
I have longings to write as fairies write.

*A*fter the chickens I did go
to feed the folks in the nursery.
The caterpillars do eat so much.
They do get hungry feels
inside them most often.
When I did have them well fed
I did make tries to get them
into their christening robes
so they can be christened
before they do grow more old
and before they do grow too big
to wear their christening robes.

The matter of making christening robes
for caterpillars is not a difficult one.
The difficulty is to get a frisky caterpillar
to keep still while one is putting on his robe.
And then it is a problem to keep it on.

Before I did get five caterpillars
into their christening robes,

I did hear the mama calling.
She did have needs of me.
I ran a quick run to the house.
When I did walk in the door
I did hold up my dress.
The mama makes me do that
so she can see if I have any animals
in the pockets I pin on my underskirts.
She has objects to animals in the house.

Then the mama did send me to pick elderberries.
She did tell me to scoot up the tree in a hurry.
I did so.
In the pasture by the pond
I did see a mother sheep.
In the pond is a lily
that does float upon the water.
I wonder how that came to be.

When the pail was all full of elderberries
I did get down.
I set the pail on a little stump.
Brave Horatius stayed to guard it
while I did go to the hilltop.
I feel like a bird sometimes.
Then I spread my arms for wings.
I nod unto the willows
and they nod unto me.
They wave their arms
and I wave mine.

And afterwards when I did get my pail
of elderberries they were gone.
They were gone only a little way.
Brave Horatius did have feelings
those elderberries ought to be
going to the house we live in.
So he did make starts with them.
When I did catch up with him
he did have the pail handle in his mouth.
He was going in a slow way.
And only a few elderberries did spill out.

The waters of the brook lap and lap.
They come in little ripples over grey stones.
They are rippling a song.
It is a goodbye song to Lars Porsena.
He is the crow that is no more.

It was only yesterday.
I was making a go across the cornfield.
Lars Porsena was going on ahead.
His movements did look queer
with his tail feathers not growed out yet.
Brave Horatius did follow after me.
The crow came back to see if we were coming.
I was watching him with joy feels in my heart.
Brave Horatius did give a queer bark
and he pulled the corner of my apron.
I looked looks about.

The chore boy was in the corner
of the cornfield with a gun.
Maybe he did not see Lars Porsena there.
I ran a quick run to stop him.
I hollered hollers at him.
When I was come to where he was
I did tell him he must not shoot that old gun.
A ball in it might go as far as Lars Porsena.

He just laughed a laugh.
He said that Lars Porsena
was nothing but a crow.
And then he pointed that gun
right at my own dear Lars Porsena.
The noise was a big awful cal lamb of tea.
I had feels I was killed dead
when I saw him fall.

I ran a quick run.
I found he was making little flutterings.
When I did pick him up
he was wet with much blood.
I felt the shivers of his pains.
I wrapped my apron around him
so he would not have cold feels.
There was much blood on it
as we did go along.

The raindrops were coming down
in a slow, sad way.
The sky was crying tears
for the hurts of Lars Porsena.
And I was too.

I had not knows what to do.
I did cuddle him up close in my arms
and I washed off some of the blood,
but more and more came
and sleepy feels were upon him.
I did sing "Sanctus, sanctus, Dominus Deus."

Now I hear the mama say
"I wonder where Opal is."
She has forgets.
I'm still under the bed
where she put me quite some time ago.
She did not have likings
for my putting Lars Porsena on my bed.

We both had sleeps together.
Only now he does not have wakeups
and stiffness is upon him.
I did have queer feels in my throat
and pain feels all up and down me.
I so did want him alive again to go explores.

*T*he clouds go slow across the sky.
No one seems to be in a hurry.
Even the wind walks slow.
I think the wind is dreaming too.
This is a dream day.

I did go to the tall fir tree.
I lay Lars Porsena near him.
I said a little prayer
and covered him over with moss.
Brave Horatius has longs for Lars Porsena
to come and perch upon his back.
He does wait waits and quiet is upon him.

*T*he new horse did have flies upon him.
They were giving Savonarola some bothers.
I took my apron and shooed some of them away.
I did have needs of the papa's newspaper.
I could make that go more far up
than I could make my apron go.
Those flies were most lazy.
They didn't want to make moves at all.

Aphrodite has likes for shower baths
I do give her out of the flower sprinkler.
She is such a nice mother pig.
First come back brushes and then more showers.
The fairies did leave this sprinkler
after I put the letter
in the moss box by the old log.
At the end of warm days
I water the wild flowers
and I water the plants
that do grow in the garden.
I can almost hear the tomato plants say,
"We were waiting for you"
every time I give them sprinkles.

*S*ome day I will write about
the great tree that I love.
Today I did watch
and I did hear its moans
as the saw went through it.
There was a queer feel in my throat
and I couldn't stand up.
All the woods seemed still
except the pain-sound of the saw.
It seemed like a little voice
was calling from the cliffs.
And then it was many voices.
They were all little voices calling
as one silver voice come together.

The saw—it didn't stop—
it went on sawing.
Then I did have thinks
the silver voice was calling
to the soul of the big tree.
The saw did stop.
There was a stillness.
There was a queer sad sound.
The big tree did quiver
It did sway.
It crashed to earth.
Oh, Michael Raphael!

*O*ne of my tooths is loose
and a queer feel.
I did go to the string box
and pulled out a string.
It was feets long.
I did tie one part of it
around my tooth with carefuls.
Then I did tie the other end
to the broom handle behind the door.
I went a walk off.

The tooth didn't come out.
The string did just slip
off the broom handle.
I carried the string
while I did go to bring in wood.

When the works was done
then I tied that string to the door knob.
I started to walk off.
Then I came back a ways.
Then I thought I'd wait until after dinner.

Yesterday was the funeral of Aristotle.
He died of eating too many mosquitoes.
Now I have not three pet bats.
I only have two.
And they are like mice with angel wings.
I have likes to watch them
scratch their heads with their hind foots.
They do use a part of their wonderful
stretchy wings for a wash cloth.
Now I go goes to the garden
to get turnips for the supper.

Today the fairies did bring
more color pencils
to the moss box by the old log.
There was a purple one and more too.
I looked looks at them.
Then I climbed up in a tree
to be more near the sky.

I did see the penseé girl
with the faraway look in her eyes

and the man of the long step
that whistles most all of the time
come walking through the woods.

It is often now they come.
And he does gather ferns for her.
They came right on
till they was by the moss box.
They did not leave a note for the fairies.
They didn't even see the box.

I had sees there was joy-lights in her eyes
and the looks he looked at her
was like the looks the young husband
of Dear Love does look at her
when he is come home from work.

He is a most strong man.
He put his arms around the penseé girl
and he most lifted her off the ground.
He did take out a ring of gold
and he did tell her it was
his mother's wedding ring.
A butterfly went by—it was a cream one
with a nice ribbon at its wing edge
and pinkish spots.

He did kiss her again.
They didn't see the green caterpillar
having sleeps under the hazel leaf.

And he did say, "I want you
to have all the love in the world."
And the fat green caterpillar
fell off the leaf away down to the ground.
And he kissed her again.
And the green caterpillar made begins
to crawl back up the hazel bush.
I breathed a big breathe of reliefs
about him not having steps on.

After they left I went for Felix Mendelssohn.
He was very near the altar of Good King Edward I.
This being the day of his crowning in 1274,
I thought I would see the little plants
was growing in a nice way.
They was.
I planted them from the woods in a spring day.
I did hope they would burst into bloom
on his crowning day
and make a crown of flowers on his altar.
But the dear little things got in a hurry
and they did bloom more than a month ago.
Now they are saying beautiful things
with their leaves.

While I was putting rocks around the altar
the man that wears grey neckties
and is kind to mice came along.
The big rocks that were too big
he did lift and place on the altar there.

And then he did help me plant mosses
in between the rocks.
That made me happy.
Men are such a blessing to have about.

Together we saw a little snake.
When I see snakes I like to stop and watch.
Their dresses fit them tight.
They can't fluff out their clothes
like birds can,
but snakes are quick people.
They move in such a pretty way.
Their eyes are bright
and their tongues are slim.

The day was most warm.
I saw the willows by the creek
dabbling their feet in the water.
Then I sat on the edge of the bank
and dabbled my toes.
One drinks in so much inspiration
with one's toes in a willow creek.
One hears the talkings of the plants
that dwell there.
My legs did have longings to go in wading
but I went not.
The mama wanted me home for works.

While I was lacing up my shoes
I saw Elizabeth Barrett Browning.
I took off my sunbonnet and tied it on her

so the sun wouldn't bother her eyes.
She was a lovely cow with the bonnet on.
And she did go her way and I did go mine.

The mama did send me with eggs
to the house of Mrs. Limberger.
From far away I saw her talking to a woman.
It was Sadie McKibben and she wore a new dress.
It had blossoms and freckles on it
like the freckles on her face
and it was beautiful.
Also did Mrs. Limberger wear a new dress.
It was black and had a yellow stripe
like unto one of those yellow stripes
the garter snake wears on his back.

They were so busy talking
that they heard me not.
I reached out the eggs.
They saw them not.
Then I did edge over to Sadie McKibben.
I gave her sleeve a little pull.
She looked down at me and smiled.
She went on talking.
She gave each one of my curls a smooth-out
while she talked on.

Then Mrs. Limberger did happen to see the eggs.
She reached and took them.
I was glad.
But my arm was the most glad part of me.

As I started home Sadie McKibben
did give me goodbye kisses on each cheek.
She knows how I do long for kisses.
and how the mama hasn't time to give me any.
When I went by Mrs. Limberger
she gave me a pat
and when she did, it went right through
my dress to Felix Mendelssohn.
He gave a squeak.
He only likes pats from me.

When I came back
the mama did spank me real hard
and told me to go and find my sunbonnet
and not to come back until I did find it.
I went to the altar of Good King Edward I to pray.
Then I went to the nursery and the hospital.
Now I do see Elizabeth Barrett Browning
and she has got my sunbonnet on.
It helped to keep the sun
from hurting her beautiful eyes.

I sit here on the doorstep
printing on this wrapping paper.
The baby is in bed asleep.
The mama and the rest of the folks
is gone to the ranch house.
She said for me to stay in the doorway
to see that nothing comes
to carry the baby away.
The back part of me feels a little bit sore,

but I am happy listening
to the twilight music
of God's good world.

I did see some flutterings on the road.
It was a very little thing
and it made little moves.
When I was come it was a little bird
that was hurt by the step of a cow.
I have thinks it was making a go across the road.
I cuddled it up
and I felt feels in my pocket
and there was mentholatum.

I did give it some applies
and we went to the hospital.
I put the bird on some moss
in a little soap box room
where nothing can come
and bring it more hurts.
It did have likes for the water
I gave it to drink in a thimble.

And more likes it did have
for the food I gave it to eat.
I named it William Makepeace Thackeray.

The mama did have me help her
take the children to the house of her mother.
They stayed there all day.
I went to visit the folks in the pasture.

It was most warm.
The folks in the pasture
were not out in the sun.
Elizabeth Barrett Browning
was under the big tree.
She did look gentle looks at me.
And I put my arm around her neck.
Her mother, the gentle Jersey cow,
was also in the shade.
She did come with me as far as the brook.
I watched her take a long drink.

I looked looks for the little bucket
I do take drinks of water in.
I found it by the willow bush.
Aphrodite does have longings for a drink
of cold water these warm days.
She did grunt grunts of appreciations.
Then she did grunt another grunt.
I have thinks the other grunt was not

to forget a drink of cold water
for the pig that does belong to the man
that our lane does belong to.

The sun—it was hot down on my head.
I took two big maple leaves
and they did some help
to keep its warmness from my head.
At the edge of the near woods
I met my dear Thomas Chatterton Jupiter Zeus,
my beautiful woodrat,
and we went on together.
I did carry him in one arm
and I did hold a maple leaf
over him with the other.

By and by there was no sun.
The warmness did have a different feel.
There were grey clouds in the sky.
Some were darkness.
I climbed the lane gate.

There was a great noise.
I wrapped my lovely woodrat in my sunbonnet.
He cuddled up against me.
The great noise came again.
I whispered to him, "Il tonne." [*a boom*]
We went on.
In between times there was fire in the sky.
It made moves a quick way.

After it was the coming of the great noise.
Every time I did whisper to Thomas Chatterton
Jupiter Zeus, "Il tonne."
I so did so he would have thinks
the great noise was something else.

At the ending of the lane
were come some very big pats of rain.
There was Brave Horatius.
He had been on looks for us.
We went on together.

On the path that does lead to our house
we did hear a calling.
It was a mournful sound.
I had thinks some little life
was much hurt and did have needs of my help.
I felt for the little box
of mentholatum in my pocket.
It was there and some bandage too.

The sound came again.
I followed after it.
Once I did have thinks it came from a root.
And then it was like it did come from a big tree.
It was a pain-voice.
It was just a voice without words.

I followed after its queer callings.
Brave Horatius followed after me.

He would stop and look
queer puzzle-looks at nowhere.
We did go on.
The voice sound came again.
It was like a voice lost
from the person it did belong to.
We were more near to it.
We followed it around a big tree.

There it was come from the man on the stump.
He did throw back his head
and the voice came out his throat
and went to nowhere.
And he did turn his face about.
It was the face of the husband
of Sadie McKibben.
But the look—the look in his eyes—
was a queer wild look that looked
looks at nowhere.

*A*fter suppertime I did have seeing
out the window of the night.
It was calling, "Petite Francoise,
come, petite Francoise."
I went.
Brave Horatius followed after.
A big yellow silver ball
was coming up over the hill.
I did climb on a rock to watch its coming.

Brave Horatius put his nose by my hand.
I gave him pats.
He looked up at me.
I told him,
"C'est la pleine lune." [*It's the full moon*]
We went on to the hill where its coming was.

*M*orning work is done.
There is enough barks in the woodbox
for today and tomorrow.
And many kindlings are on the floor.
Now I can make prints.

I am sitting on a log for the last time
in my cathedral.
Tomorrow we will move to a mill town.
Elizabeth Barrett Browning has been sold
with her mother, the gentle Jersey.

The mama does say
none but my necessary things can go.

She said that was my blue calico apron
and my grey calico apron
and the clothes that goes under them
and my two pairs of stockings
and the shoes I have on
and my sunbonnet
and my slate
and Cyr's Reader.

But I have more necessary things
that the mama has not knows of.
There is my two books that Angel Mother
and Angel Father did write in,
and the pictures of grandmere and grandpere,
and the lily plant
that the soul of Peter Paul Rubens
does love to be near,
and the bath towel
of Thomas Chatterton Jupiter Zeus
that Dear Love made for him,
and the color pencils from the fairies,
and the track of Elizabeth Barrett Browning,
and the string I pulled my tooth with,
and the tail feathers of Lars Porsena,
and the egg shells Sir Francis Bacon
and Oliver Goldsmith hatched out of,
and the portraits of my friends on poker chips,
and Solomon Grundy's christening robe,
and four horse shoes of William Shakespeare.

The man who wears grey neckties
and is kind to mice
is going to take care of my mouse friends
in his bunkhouse.

Dear Love and her husband
say Virgil can live
under their front step.
They will also watch over my hospital.

I have walked past the house
of the girl who has no seeing
and I prayed prayers.
I will leave letters for the fairies
in the moss box by the old log.

When I was come for the last time
to the house of Dear Love
she was sitting on the steps
drying her hair in the sun.
It did wave little ripples of light.
She let me have feels of its touches
and she did give me a last kiss on each cheek.
When I told her that Sadie McKibben
also gives me one on the nose
she so did as she
lifted me onto her lap.

Then Dear Love did tell me a secret.
Only her husband knows.

And now I know.
They are going to have a baby in five months.
The angels let them know ahead.

I felt a big amount of satisfaction.
It is about time that prayer was answered.
Some prayers you pray a little while
and answers come.
Some prayers you pray more times
and answers don't come.
I have not knows of why.
But prayers for babies
most always get answered soon.

POSTSCRIPT

AFTERWORD

THE CAST OF
CHARACTERS IN
OPAL'S WORLD

Opal spent nine months piecing together her childhood diary.

POSTSCRIPT

OPAL WHITELEY

May 1920

Of the days before I was taken to the lumber camps there is little I remember. As piece by piece the journal comes together, some things come back. There are references here and there in the journal to things I saw or heard or learned in those days before I came to the lumber camps.

There were walks in the fields and woods. When on these walks, Mother would tell me to listen to what the flowers and trees and birds were saying. We listened together. And on the way she told me poems and other lovely things, some of which she wrote in the two books and also in others which I had not with me in the lumber camps. On the walks, and after we came back, she had me to print what I had seen and what I had heard. After that she told me of different people and their wonderful work on earth. Then she would have me tell again to her what she had told me. After I came to the lumber camp,

I told these things to the trees and the brooks and the flowers.

There were five words my mother said to me over and over again, as she had me to print what I had seen and what I had heard. These words were: What, Where, When, How, Why. They had a very great influence over all my observations and the recording of those observations during all of my childhood. And my Mother having put such strong emphasis on these five words accounts for much of the detailed descriptions that are throughout my diary.

No children I knew. There were only Mother and the kind woman who taught me and looked after me and dressed me, and the young girl who fed me. And there was Father in those few days when he was home from the far lands. Those were wonderful days—his home-coming days. Then he would take me on his knee and ride me on his shoulders and tell me of the animals and birds of far lands. And we went for many walks, and he would talk to me about many things along the way. It was then he taught me Comparer.

There was one day when I went with Mother in a boat. It was a little way on the sea. It was a happy day. Then something happened and we were all in the water. Afterwards, when I called for Mother, they said the sea waves had taken her and she was gone to heaven. I remember the day because I never saw my Mother again.

The time was not long after that day with Mother in the boat when the kind woman who took care of me did tell me gently that Father too had gone to heaven while he was away in the far lands. She said she was going to take me to the mother and father of my Father—grandmere and grandpere.

We started. But I never got to see my dear grandmother and grandfather whom I had never seen. Something happened on the way and I was all alone. And I didn't feel happy. There were strange people that I had never seen before—and I was afraid of them. They made me to keep very still and we went for no walks in the field. But we travelled a long, long way.

Then it was they put me with Mrs. Whiteley. The day they put me with her was a rainy day and I thought she was a little afraid of them too. She took me on the train and in a stage coach to the lumber camp. She called me Opal Whiteley, the name of a girl the same size as I was when her mother lost her. She took me into the camp as her own child and so called me as we lived in the different lumber camps and in the mill towns.

With me I took into camp a small box. In a slide drawer in the bottom of this box were two books which my own Mother and Father (the Angel Mother and Father I always speak of in my diary) had written in. I do not think the people who put me with Mrs. Whiteley knew about the books, for they took everything out of the top part of the box and tossed it aside. I picked it up and kept it with me, and being as I was more quiet with it in my arms, they allowed me to keep the box, thinking it was empty.

These books I kept always with me until one day I shall always remember when I was about twelve years old and they were taken from my hiding place in the woods. Day by day I had spelled over and over the many words that were written in them. It was the many little things recorded there that helped me to remember what my Mother and Father had already told me of different great lives and their work. They made me very eager to be learning more and more of what was recorded in them, and I studied them much more than I did my books at school. Their influence on my life has been great.

This diary is of my fifth and sixth year. Far on into other years I continued it and perhaps some other time the story will be pieced together and made into another book.

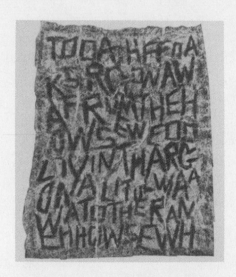

This diary page was written on a paper bag. It says, "Today the folks are gone away from the house we do live in. They are gone a little way away to the ranch house wh"

AFTERWORD

JANE BOULTON
February 1984

Unfortunately for us, the rest of Opal's diary was not pieced together, and the entries for the following years were not published.

The putting-together of the first part alone represented an enormous labor. As Ellery Sedgwick described it: "After urging her to send for the pieces, they came. There were hundreds, thousands, one might say millions of them. Some few were large as a half sheet of notepaper, more, scarce big enough to hold a letter of the alphabet. The paper was of all shades, sorts and sizes: butcher's bags pressed and sliced in two, wrapping paper, the backs of envelopes—anything and everything that could hold writing. The early years are printed in letters so close that, when the sheets are printed, not another letter can be squeezed in."

Sedgwick also wrote of Opal's puzzlement over "letters that would not shape into familiar phrases." Turning to her editors, she was told that the words were French.

"They can't be French! I never studied French," she protested. But French they were.

For nine months she put the scraps together like a giant puzzle. With a methodical thoroughness that would have brought credit to a museum, she created a system of cards onto which the diary pieces were transferred. Her childish adornment of page borders had been fortunate, enabling her to reconstruct whole pages from the fragments. Because she had used each colored pencil until it was gone, incidents which followed one another could be connected sequentially. When the work was completed, Ellery Sedgwick described it as "the journal of an understanding heart."

Early in her life Opal decided her calling was to teach children about the many creatures she loved. Further study about the plants and animals she had observed required a college education. By washing, picking berries, and doing all sorts of rough work, she was able to buy books. Hardship was nothing new to her. In 1916 she entered the University of Oregon where she considered it insignificant to live in a room without furniture other than a two dollar cot and two coats for blankets.

Professors were amazed at her advanced comprehension of botany and geology. "This experience happens to a university but once in a generation" declared Warren D. Smith, head of the Geology Department. "She knows more about geology than do many students who have graduated from my classes. She may become one of the greatest minds Oregon has ever produced."

"Her work was never scientific," said Dr. John Bovard, head of the Zoology Department, under whom Opal studied bird life. "She is a child in her mind still and extremely imaginative. She is a genius in her way."

Before the school year was finished, "the mama," Mrs. Whiteley, died. Opal dropped out of college, borrowed money from friends, and went south to Los Angeles to seek her livelihood by giving nature lessons to children. Her perseverance and some opportune introductions to people of means led to success with this venture. These same supporters helped her raise money for the publication of her own nature book, *The Fairyland Around Us.* Though her personal canvass produced the prodigious sum of $9,400, its sequel was not so bright. The printers demanded $10,000, and since the additional $600 was not forthcoming, they despaired of their young girl client and destroyed the plates.

A serious illness followed which hospitalized her. Again, merciful friends, attracted to the warmhearted girl, came to her assistance. Eventually well, at the age of twenty-one, she travelled eastward to find a publisher for her ill-fated *Fairyland.* It was then that she met the *Atlantic Monthly* editor who was to discover her diary.

Living in the home of Mrs. Walter Cabot, the mother-in-law of Ellery Sedgwick, during the long months it took to piece the diary together, she met many important people. Among them was Lord Grey of Fallodon, who was later to write the foreword for the

British edition of *The Diary of Opal Whiteley*. Then Chief Justice of the Supreme Court, Charles Evans Hughes, and his wife took the young girl to London.

For more than five years Opal had frequented my thoughts—ever since a friend had loaned me the original limited edition of her diary. Impressed, I had sent fragments of the work to *Ms.* magazine where they appeared in April 1975. Among the letters that poured in from new Opal fans was one from Amanda Vaill, an editor at Macmillan Publishing Company in New York. "Would it be possible," she wrote, "to expand this wonderful fragment into a book-length manuscript?"

Although the *Atlantic Monthly* no longer had files on Opal or her whereabouts, from a scholar in Massachusetts I learned of a woman who had corresponded with the diarist in 1969. At that time Opal was a patient in a hospital outside London where she had been taken when authorities discovered her near starvation, unable to care for herself, having used money that friends had given her for books rather than food.

My correspondence followed with hospital administrators until one finally answered, "The lady you call Opal Whiteley is known to us as Francoise D'Orleans, and is indeed alive and here."

At that, Opal's words came back to me from the diary: "After suppertime I did have seeing out the window of the night. It was calling, 'Petite Francoise, come, petite Francoise.' "

In October 1975, joined by my closest friend, I left my home on a sheep ranch in Alberta, Canada, to fly to England to see Opal. Considering that she was nearing eighty, we did not know what to expect. But she came toward us in little running steps, her face eager, even radiant, with expressive brown eyes and winged eyebrows. How tiny she was. Less than five feet tall.

"So good of you to come. I have your letter, but you didn't say how many sheep you have." Opal took both my hands into her own small ones as the words poured out. She was grateful for visitors, hungry for fresh fruit, and anxious to talk about her life.

Hearing how her diary had reached so many hearts made her glow with pleasure. When asked about her parents, she explained her discovery that her father was the French naturalist and author, Henri, Duc D'Orleans. She had met his mother (her grandmother), the Duchess of Chartres, who had financed Opal's trip to India to retrace Henri's travels. Our heroine was never to see her again because the Duchess died while Opal was in India, but from that time on she called herself Francoise D'Orleans.

Ellery Sedgwick found proof of this trip to India through letters from two maharajas describing "a series of fetes given to do her honour," and Opal's own account of the journey written in articles for *The Queen* in 1929.

Opal (Francoise) never married, never had children, and all her early writings were lost to her. In London, to learn more about her parents, she bought every book available on genealogy, but because she was institutionalized, they too were taken away. A benevolent friend, The Honorable Mrs. Woodruff, has helped pay storage costs all these long years on 483 boxes of books.

"Is it possible to go through Opal's books in storage?" I asked this generous woman. "It will depress you terribly, I fear," she answered. "They are the most pitiful of possessions. Book experts say they have no value at all."

When I questioned Mrs. Woodruff about the authenticity of Opal's claim to royal parents, she said, "Others before you have tried to trace her heritage. Some people in Oregon maintain she was not adopted. Of this I am sure: no six-year-old child of an Oregon lumberman could have named French trees and rivers and produced a diary where she thought and wrote in a French construction. Although we do not know what she is, we absolutely know what she is not."

In snapshots Opal looked like the other Whiteley children, but Europeans commented on her uncanny resemblance to the French royalty of that day. "She might just as easily have been the great-great-granddaughter of the last King of France," Mrs. Woodruff added.

As to the heritage Opal claims, there is a documented family tree of the House of France. Louis Phillipe, Duke of Orleans, abdicated in 1848 and fled to England as "Mr. Smith." His eldest son was Ferdinand Phillipe Louis Charles Henri, Duke of Orleans, who had a son named Robert, Duke of Chartres (the "Grandpere" of the diary). Robert married his cousin, Francoise Marie Amelia ("Grandmere" of the diary) and it was their son, Henri, whom Opal claims as "Angel Father."

"Henri Duc D'Orleans," states a French encyclopedia, "was born in Ham near Richmond 1867. At 22 started a long trip to Central Asia with Bonvalot that earned him the Grand Medal of the Geographic Society in 1890. Made an exploration 1892 into Oriental Africa. 1895 went with Briffaut from Hanoi to Calcutta. Died in Saigon in 1901 at age of 34." (Since no record of her birth was ever found, we can only estimate that Opal was born about 1898.)

It was never established if the Duke married or produced an heir, but Elizabeth Bradburne (now Lawrence) wrote in her book, *Opal Whiteley: the Unsolved Mystery,* published in England in 1962 (Putnam), that following the grave revolutionary events of 1896 anyone of royal blood might be a center of unrest and embarrassment. There would be even more reason for removing a child from the scene if she were illegitimate.

She pondered how a daughter of the Whiteleys could be so conversant with the Roman Catholic Church, baptizing her pets in the wooded cathedral where she sang the Angelus and Ave Maria to them. "This would seem to come from the heart," she wrote, "from a familiarity with Catholic ritual such as could be experienced only by someone raised through early childhood in that atmosphere. If the idea of foster parents were an illusion, how was so young a child able to draw on a culture wholly foreign to her actual background?"

What a different story comes from the people in Oregon who refused to believe Opal's aristocratic ties. Some insisted she was not adopted. Among them was Grandma Scott, mother of the one we know as "the mama." Interviewed by Fred Lockley in *The Bookman,* April 1921, her answers were querulous: "Why does she want to disown her own folks? I'll tell you, Mister, there's no mystery about it. I never did understand Opal. She used to tell awful lies when she was little about what toads and birds said to her, just as if toads and birds could talk. Switching her didn't seem to do much good. When I would talk to her she would look at me as solemn as an owl and when I was all through, she'd say, 'What did you say? I was thinking about something else.' And I'd have to spank her all over again. I'm glad the other children aren't like Opal, for she was very trying."

This same Grandma Scott was helpful to the research of Elizabeth Bradburne, identifying some twenty persons mentioned in the diary: the girl with no seeing burned to death in the manner described; Opal climbed a large tree when she was sad; the husband of Sadie McKibben did go crazy, and both the pet crow and grey horse died as written.

Elbert Bede, editor of the local paper in Cottage Grove, Oregon, who knew Opal personally, spent many years investigating her story. In his *Fabulous Opal*

Whiteley (Binfords and Mort 1954) he wrote: "Opal was an odd child and the only member of the family with an unusually developed love for nature. In so many ways she was different from the Whiteleys that, without supporting evidence for the Whiteley parentage, her story might be convincing."

In the end skeptical, Bede's premise was that the diary was substantially rewritten before Opal was twenty. Ellery Sedgwick asserted this to be impossible since he and his family were constantly with her while she was piecing together the scraps to prepare the manuscript.

If one is to believe Bede's theory, it must follow that Opal went through the immense labor of printing thousands of words in childish capitals, carefully misspelling most of them. Having done this formidable work, Opal would have had to tear into bits each page to store as a hoax in a cardboard box. If she found these childhood notes in college and wrote from them the story we know, its tender memoirs would be just as authentically hers—unforgetable, if not so precocious. But it is difficult to picture this guileless child going through such a prolonged process before she had even met Ellery Sedgwick who was to ask about the diary.

Some would not let it rest there. Experts were called in to examine the diary scraps microscopically. "The paper," wrote Bradburne, "was found to be a particular kind manufactured only before World War I." Further microscopic evidence revealed that the pages had been exposed to effects of damp weather, which would corroborate Opal's explanation of their being hidden in the woods.

Primarily interested in child development, Bradburne noted colored frames on some of Opal's pages which psychologists later explained as a feature most typical in the writings of maladjusted or insecure children. The frame is a sort of fence to surround and protect them from the world.

In Opal's diary (not included in my adaptation) she describes a song: "When we were come to the bridge, we made a stop and did sing to the riviere a song. I sang it the Chant de Seine, de Havre, et Essone et Nonette et Roullon et Iron et Darnetal et Ourcq et Rille et Loing et Eure et Audelle et Nonette et Sarc. I sang it as Angel Father did teach me to, and as he has wrote in the book."

To all appearances this recitation is a random collection of French rivers. Yet one day a reader called to Ellery Sedgwick's attention the fact that the first letter of each river (after Seine) spells the name of HENRI D'ORLEANS, and they were all rivers surrounding the D'Orleans home.

"Only later," wrote Bradburne, "was it found that the D'Orleans family enjoyed anagrams and rhymes of this kind," concluding that Opal learned these strings of names in childhood without realizing their significance.

"What adds weight to the evidence," she continued, "is the fact that there are mistakes in some of the lists. Sometimes a name is omitted, which breaks the sequence, or another substituted. This seems like the natural inaccuracy of a child." If these lists were added later to the diary, she would surely have insured their exactness.

"The diarist was correct," wrote Elbert Bede, "when she said she had never studied French." He personally checked the library files to determine that she had withdrawn no French textbooks or dictionaries.

Meantime, Ellery Sedgwick continued to put his own pieces together. In his book, *The Happy Profession*, he tells of letters continuing to pour in twenty-five years after Opal's diary was published. "What Opal may have come to believe is a very different matter from the question of the veracity of the journal of this child of fancy. Of the rightness and honesty of the manuscript as *The Atlantic Monthly* printed it, I am utterly convinced; more certain am I than of the authorship of many another famous diary, for I have watched the original copy reborn and subjected to the closest scrutiny."

His interpretations went further: "At the heart of every little girl Cinderella sits enthroned, and with Opal the legend grew to be true, and the truth magnified with the years, finally permeating her entire life."

While some explored its veracity, the literary world was examining its value. The chairman of the English house of Putnam who published her book wrote: "Miss Whiteley's book I regard as a very remarkable work of genius, ranking with the great works of all time."

Christopher Morley in the *New York Evening Post* wrote: "There will be a local controversy by and by, we dare say, about *The Story of Opal*. Already there is a row on about it in England. The argument seems to be not whether it is genuine, but whether it is literature. H.M. Tomlinson finds Opal's diary one more disheartening proof that Americans are a 'fantastically sentimental race,' while it seems to us to have the 'innocence of the eye' that Santayana considers the essence of poetry."

The story is long and involved—one whose mystery we shall never solve. But her work of strange beauty stands. Let those who will say she is not from royal blood. Let those who will say she could not have written this diary as a child of six. But the diary *is* hers, and there has been time for nothing else in her life but this obsessive dream—to find the mother and father who lived in her child heart.

Jane Boulton

February 1984

THE CAST OF
CHARACTERS IN
OPAL'S WORLD

and the pages on which they appear

189